Womanheart®

To Deanna,
A lady of light
and high purpose,
Shine on!!
Blessings,
Jangeet ♡

Sangeet Kaur Khalsa

Womanheart®

Healing Our Relationships,
Loving Ourselves

Keep Up! Publishing

PUBLISHED BY KEEP UP! PUBLISHING
Phoenix, Arizona, USA
Call: (800) 499-4024 or
Email: info@keepuppublishing.com

First American edition published in 2002
by Keep Up! Publishing.

1 3 5 7 9 10 8 6 4 2

Keep Up! and the portrayal of a person with up-stretched arms
are a trademark of Keep Up! Publishing

"Walk This World" by Heather Nova
(C) Big Live Music America, Inc.

Cover photo and photos in the *Resources to Explore* chapter
by Hari Nam Singh.

Cover design and layout by Liv Singh Khalsa.

Illustrations by Barbara Rutledge.

IMPORTANT:
BEFORE ENGAGING IN ANY EXERCISE, INCLUDING THOSE
THAT MAY BE IN THIS PUBLICATION, CONSULT YOUR
HEALTH CARE PROFESSIONAL. THIS PUBLICATION IS NOT
INTENDED TO PROVIDE MEDICAL ADVICE NOR IS IT
INTENDED AS A SUBSTITUTE FOR ANY TREATMENT
PRESCRIBED BY YOUR HEALTH CARE PROFESSIONAL.

DEDICATION

This book is dedicated to my teacher and friend, Yogi Bhajan, the Master of Kundalini Yoga and White Tantric Yoga and the spiritual leader of the Sikh path in the Western Hemisphere.

For more than 30 years he has taught the science of the possible human known as Humanology, teaching women especially each summer at Khalsa Women's Training Camps in New Mexico.

Much of the understanding he imparted to us in the early teachings in the late '70s and early '80s forms the principle backbone of this book. Through these teachings I, and thousands of other women, came to learn how to live a life of excellence and grace in harmony with others.

Each day I live I thank God for his contributions to all women.

Womanheart®
Healing Our Relationships, Loving Ourselves

ACKNOWLEDGMENTS

This book would not have been possible without the assistance, support and inspiration of dozens of people, many of whom currently serve on my healing staff and Womanheart Retreat staff, and who also are clients and students in many of my classes.

Most importantly, I want to acknowledge the enormous inspiration, patience and help in design, editing and printing provided by my business partner and good friend, Hari Nam Singh. No one I know could have served this process, the larger mission of Womanheart itself, or me personally, better than he has.

I bless all of you in the name of beloved God.

INTRODUCTION

To All Dear Woman Hearts:

First things first –
What is this thing called "Womanheart?"

Womanheart is a term that covers many things. It is a state of being – of being kind and compassionate, courageous and conscious. It is a way of life, a path we as women walk, *"the way of excellence and grace."*

To those women close to me over the past nine years who know the term most personally, Womanheart is a process they engaged in when they first entered a teaching program I created by that name.

The concept of Womanheart came through me in a waking vision at literally the dawn of the Year 1991. Its roots grew from the ancient lineage of wisdom taught by yogic masters as "the art of the Oriental Woman" which I learned from the wisest man now living on Earth, Yogi Bhajan, the Master of Kundalini and White Tantric yogas.

Over thirty years of teaching men and women of all ages here in the West, focusing his work with women in summer retreats in New Mexico, USA, he defined the teachings that inspired me to live joyfully as a woman for the first time in my life.

My journey up to that point had been outwardly successful and inwardly painful.

In 1979 I emerged from the grime of the corporate executive jungle, where I had all but become a man, to discover within me the meditative power and compassionate grace that God intended for me to experience. The mysticism of my childhood had finally found a home.

It would take several years of training and growth in yogic lifestyles, however, for me to gain and test my courage, and even more to come to the point where I could teach not just from my teacher's teachings but from those which God directed through me as a counselor, healer and teacher. I reached that point in the summer of 1995 when I came back to New Mexico to teach at the same family of women's retreats that had taught me so much years before.

In my growth process between those years, I had undergone a major transformation. I had thrown off pain and disease, the threat of a wheelchair existence, and a neediness for men, money and power, and had traded in my faith in God for direct knowledge and the experience of the God-in-me and the God-through-me present in all of us.

The route of enlightenment for us all – women and men – is simple: to learn from our teachers, to live our excellence, to discover the teacher within us and live by that command, to love without attachment to expectations or outcomes, and when the time comes to gracefully go Home, shining a light for others to follow.

There are no guarantees that any one of us will complete this path in this lifetime, but the way Home is open to us all, and in some lifetime we will all so deliver ourselves.

Men and women together must lead themselves to this deliverance. But what is the role for women?

For centuries men have been trained in leadership skills, but they could not deliver the world to peace and harmony, and certainly not working by themselves alone. Now it remains for us as women to also take up the lead – not as pseudo-men, but as women trained to lead from the heart as well as from the head, from compassion as well as from consciousness.

For women this is a noble path rarely walked, for we have been taught that our hearts make us weak and enslave us. Nothing could be farther from the truth.

For the heart has its own unique power, a power which can free us from slavery – slavery that has engulfed men as well as women.

This book is written to help women walk this most noble path. It speaks of the soul of Womanheart and what it takes to live on this path. This book is full of stories about women I have been proud to help walk along this path.

S. S. Sangeet Kaur Khalsa
September 11, 2000

Womanheart®

1

THE CIRCLE OF WOMEN

Why fear?
The sound current we have
created is a mighty force field
and cannot be broken.

We are protected.
We are in the garden of God.

The Circle of Women

It is a beautiful Spring evening in my garden. The hot Phoenix sun has set and the aroma of nearby roses fills the air. The full moon has just moved above the horizon and is bathing us in silvery light.

I am sitting and chanting in a circle of remarkable women. They are remarkable not for some particular thing they have accomplished in life, but for what they are accomplishing by being here chanting this healing chant together in this circle each full moon night, month after month, year after year. They are working to grow their lives better and stronger and to share their love and light with each other.

We began our chant a few moments ago and already each woman's voice has become steadier. Their voices are beginning to blend together.

The chant is thousands of years old, from the ancient yogic tradition. It is used to take someone through a healing process, whether physical, mental, emotional or spiritual. Each month on the night of the full moon we gather, just as women have gathered for centuries, to raise our voices in unison and enlighten our lives with the power of God living and flowing within us.

This is the circle of wise women. The sacred space where all within are protected and elevated.

Several have chosen to lie in the middle of the circle to receive the healing energy directly for some affliction, physical or otherwise. A few are lying here in the circle as surrogates for others who could not attend. Their work is to receive the energy, while we around the circle draw it in, allowing some to flow through us while the rest flows out to the others.

It is a simple, beautiful process, this meditation, this prayer in action.

We are here not just for ourselves and those we know and love. We are here for our entire generation, and for those unborn yet to come. This is our way of being Divine in form.

I feel the warmth swelling in my chest as my heart center expands far beyond its earthly bounds. It is a familiar friend, this energy that flows in through my head and always expands my heart first. At some point it becomes so expanded my body no longer exists as hard substance but becomes a glowing, transparent lightforce, a shimmering being through which the cosmic wind blows and spreads out over all around me.

I watch each woman around and within this circle begin to glow in her own celestial presence.

A half-hour from now, as earthly time will measure it, we will be done - "cooked," charged up and renewed. Even the Earth will reflect the work we have done, heating up for several hundred feet around us in all directions. It will take several hours for that heat to dissipate. The night sky will glow with the dancing energy, a beam shooting miles up from us and deep down into the Earth.

We are about ten minutes into the meditation now and the voices are fully blended into one. My two ordinary eyes have long been closed. Instead, my vision is centered behind my "third eye" in the middle of my forehead, the meditative doorway that expands consciousness outward to infinity. I am about to take that great leap when something startling stops me.

Another light is dancing across my third eye, an eerie red light that captures my attention. This light is not from an etheric source. It is a small circular red spot centered directly on my forehead.

Immediately, earthly knowing jumps into my consciousness and I realize that I have become the targeted center of a rifle's laser-red scope. It even jiggles slightly with the nervous shake of the hand holding the gun.

I open my eyes and follow the red beam, spotting a small dark human form crouched on the ground under the bushes at the edge of my garden. I watch as the person swings the sight around the circle of faces and brings it back to me. There is a light touch on my elbow and I turn to see the worried face of Nancy who has also seen what is happening.

She is terrified, too shocked to even speak. Her eyes ask a dozen questions. Yes, I know what it is, I respond with my eyes, while nodding my head affirmatively. "Just keep chanting," I whisper between the voices of the others. "God is with us." She closes her eyes and continues the chant.

"There is nothing to fear; just continue the chant," the voice inside me commands. No one else is threatened. I am the only target. It is because I am different. I wear the turban of the Sikh and I stand out. Why fear? The sound current we have created is a mighty force field and cannot be broken. We are protected. We are in the garden of God.

I know I should feel fear, but as I search inside myself, inside the usual closet of fears and other feelings, there is only a deep calm. "Yea, though I walk through the valley of the shadow of death... Thou art with me..." I hear the familiar words of the 23rd Psalm inside me, mingling with the tones I am chanting.

I look outside again and I see the dark figure has moved and is crouched on the low wall between this garden and the next. The rifle and its scope are still aimed directly at me.

This is a young boy, I am told. He thinks it is a game. He is afraid of me and of what is happening here, and of what this circle of chanting women is all about. The power we are projecting has drawn him and he wants to come closer, but he is afraid of our power. He stalks by night what he fears by day. Light confronts him. He has been abused often in the light. So he seeks the power of anonymity and night.

Men have hurt him, beaten him, told him to stop crying and grow up before his time, and women have not been strong enough to protect him from that rage. He seeks the protection of powerful women and he also rages at it. Why were they not there for him when he needed them? He does not know how to communicate that, except with the force men have shown him how to use.

A hundred times in his mind he has pulled the trigger of this, his father's gun. Someday he knows he will do it for real – a day he both longs for and fears.

I continue meditating and this awareness flows through me.

Moments later he has retreated to the roof of a distant shed down the alley and the red light is off. I look around the circle at the shining, beloved faces of these women.

"Next time, you will take precautions," the voice inside me commands. "One or two women will be designated as watchers." But who can I tell of this? They look to me as their teacher and they will be frightened. "Only a few can handle it at this time. You know who they are."

I saw two faces immediately as I scanned the circle – two women who had battled their fears many times, won, and had learned to trust Creator.

I will help build more women of such courage, I promise Spirit. We will grow strong as well as sweet and wise.

The meditation is almost done now. The golden glow from this circle extends up into the night sky more than a mile. Its sweetness blankets this city and reaches out to other orbs of light in nearby hamlets, networking across this land and spreading out around the planet to lighten the darkness, to feed the hungry souls and still the hearts of hate and war.

In the words of the prayer I lead at the close of the circle, I find myself asking for blessings on all frightened children. Yes, I whisper to myself, bless especially the child up on that not-so-distant roof.

Nancy turns and looks at me with disbelief and then lowers her head, nodding with relief.

She and I will be among the half-dozen or so people who will keep the events of this night a secret for several years. It would be quite some time before I could tell this story to the others. By that time they would not be frightened.

They would have grown considerably in the strength of the work we had begun here. They would have tested their courage many times and that courage would make their lives exemplary. They would be women of compassion and consciousness. They would walk the way of excellence and grace, with gratitude for all things and judgment against none.

And years later, when they would hear the events of this night, they would be proud to have stood their ground in prayer. Proud to have gone through the Valley of Death together.

Together in the garden of God we know as life.

Together in the heart of God we call Womanheart.

2

IN THE BEGINNING

*The mother must deliver the soul
into this world with the
utmost peace and harmony.*

*It may be the most awesome
responsibility given anyone.*

In The Beginning

The influences on the child begin while he or she is in the womb. As Yogi Bhajan has explained the process, the soul is drawn to its parents through the vibrations from them that will enable the soul to address its karmic lessons in this lifetime. It enters the mother's womb on the 120th day.

From that point on, the soul becomes rooted in finite self, or unit consciousness, quickly loosing awareness of infinite consciousness from which it came.

Many of the descriptions in this chapter are drawn directly or indirectly from Yogi Bhajan's training systems for certifying Kundalini Yoga teachers, based on the ancient sciences he has taught for over 30 years.

The course of life is meant to bring many opportunities to allow the soul, atma in Sanskrit, to again become aware of infinite consciousness – that which is called God or the paramatma, great soul – and to reunite with it while yet alive.

For such a blissful union to occur while the person is still alive, the person would have to have taken up the soul's destiny path – living in God's will for the soul. Instead, the soul walks the path of karma, addressing the lessons it yearns to work out in this lifetime. If the soul follows the destiny path, that person is said to be "liberated" from the wheel of karma, and actual physical death will have no defeat over the soul. This means the soul can go Home, ending the karmic cycle of birth and rebirth. This is a great challenge and a rare event.

The soul chooses the longitude and latitude of its birth, the time of birth, and its mother. The energy of the mother determines the quality of soul she draws in, and the harmony with which that soul enters the world is determined by the environment she maintains from the 120th day since conception through to delivery.

All souls enter life with ten "bodies" or energy fields of varying density that carry specific information, convey skills and talents, and perform specific functions. One of them everyone sees and knows: the physical body. Other bodies, such as the aura, can be seen by some with trained eyes.

During the time the soul is in the womb, the mother's physical body and her consciousness are helping to form most of these energy bodies. When life ends, only one body is permanent, the "subtle body," which acts like a magic carpet to carry the soul between and through its various lifetimes. The subtle body keeps each individual soul distinct from the Great Soul. It carries within it all the records of experiences, karma and destiny that each soul has accumulated throughout its lifetimes. The mother's energy during her term of pregnancy helps set the quality of all the other nine bodies.

The first body, known as the soul body brings compassion, humility, and a strong sense of self-identity. Without the proper development in the womb, the soul could enter life with poor self-identity, be overly egotistical or lack compassion.

The second body, known as the negative mind, isn't really negative at all. It bring major assessment skills which are necessary components of one's energy field. It must be nurtured to be able to make wise choices in partners and assess risks, a lack in either ability creating profound repercussions throughout life.

The third body, or positive mind, gives the soul the ability to see possibilities, to be creative and nurturing and socially adept. Without these qualities the individual would be withdrawn and stuck.

To be able to love without condition, to be non-reactive and able to stay neutral and to be capable of the highest meditative states the soul must be accompanied by a strong fourth body, or neutral mind.

The fifth body, the actual physical body, gives us strength, flexibility and the ability to know our own excellence and experience the flow of God through us.

Once we pass into the energy fields beyond the physical body, the subtler energy bodies possess many important qualities.

There must be the self-confidence and strong immune system of the sixth, or arc body, which crowns the head, the powerful shielding effect of the seventh, or aura body, which can bring either self-reliance or propel the individual into hermit-like existence. Within the aura body comes the energizing power of the eighth, or pranic body, which carries with it the knowledge of the number of breaths the soul has in each lifetime.

The role of the ninth body, the subtle body that we said earlier carries the soul from lifetime to lifetime, is inherently the body that brings one to mastery. It brings the knowledge of how to complete things, how to have the staying power to master anything, and how to live with gratitude. And lastly, there is the natural courage and leadership power that comes with a strong tent, or radiant body.

Now understand the power given to the Mother to mold all these energies and qualities while the soul is carried in her womb.

Without her steadying input on the womb-held soul, woundings can occur on all physical, emotional and mental levels. Yet, with her help, even a soul with the most difficult karmic lessons, can have considerable strengths to meet its challenges.

The mother must deliver the soul into this world with the utmost peace and harmony. It may be the most awesome responsibility given anyone. For this reason, she was given all the skills and abilities necessary to create the perfect environment around her.

That is why the old science has told us that every woman is born with all the elements of the universe in her so that she can fulfill her role as environmental protector for humanity. She does this everywhere she goes, whether or not she has actually cradled another soul within her.

The act alone of desiring a child – choosing to get pregnant as compared to accidentally getting pregnant – can draw a higher-yearning soul. That doesn't mean that accidents, which occur in a happy family, don't also bring high souls. The soul drawn to happiness and harmony can also judge when the mother is ready to receive, even if the mother herself did not consciously draw the soul in.

When the woman realizes she is pregnant, millions of thoughts cross her mind – almost all reflecting her expectations. Will the baby be healthy and "normal" – whatever that means? Will it be a boy or girl? Will it be more like her or like her mate? Will the family be able to afford the costs of raising the child? Will there be troubles?

Thanks to advances in medical science, the mother can now know whether the child will be a boy or girl. No matter what she discovers, she starts to relate to that child differently. Hopes for having a boy or girl now come together with her beliefs about one sex or the other. Those beliefs, with their related attitudes and fears, transfer directly to the fetus.

The first and most pervasive thought forms the fetus senses translate into the rough equivalent of "I am wanted" or "I am not wanted." These first impressions can have a lifelong impact.

"I was about 22 years old when I had my first pre-natal recall."

The woman talking to me is in her late 40s and we have gone back in her emotional history to uncover deep causes for some of her negative thought patterns. This is not a trance session, though we are using anchoring and reimprinting techniques with trance-like language.

"I remember I was in my apartment and it was about 3 a.m. I had been awake most of the night, unable to sleep, though I didn't know why. So I was up writing. Then, all at once, I felt my face flushing and I had this strange desire to walk. Without hardly thinking at all, I found myself out in the hallway, just walking down to the garbage disposal and then walking back and forth a few times, almost like a robot.

"As I was walking, I realized that my skin felt sensitive, irritated. It hurt. I went inside to the bathroom and when I saw my face in the mirror I was shocked. It was all red, and so was my body, like it had been rubbed raw and irritated, yet I hadn't been rubbing myself.

"Then thoughts started coming to me. I closed my eyes and I could feel myself in a warm, moist sack being jostled around, and I realized I was in my mother's womb. I could feel her thoughts. She was angry, very angry. It was about me. I was afraid. I felt I wasn't wanted. She was shouting, and it was about me.

"I was aware that her anger had been directed at me for many weeks. Why? Why? The thoughts came through. She hated me. I was going to be a boy, she was sure of that. And she'd rather I be dead than be born a boy. And now here, just moments before birth, all the anger came spilling out of her and I was feeling it. I wasn't even struggling to get out, it was just her muscles trying to push me out. I was pulling back, so afraid of what I was coming out to be part of, what Godzilla would be my God, my parent...

"When I opened my eyes I was sitting on my couch crying and quaking from head to toe. All my life my mother had told me how very much I had been wanted, how her pregnancy was deliberately planned. And now, here in a few moments, I lived through the truth and discovered her lie.

"I couldn't wait until it was late enough in the morning to call her and ask her about the details leading up to my birth. Not about her emotions – I knew she had little or no idea about them. I just wanted the details to confirm some things, and the rest I knew. Had she really been angry and walking? Was I born about 3:30 in the morning?

"Later she told me that they had made her walk a lot because I wasn't coming out. She was so heavy with me and so upset and, because she was older, nearly 40,

they didn't want to induce labor. So they made her walk a long time, propped up between Dad and a male nurse. She laughed and said she'd have been happy to give birth to anything, just to relieve the pain. She was so grateful when she finally delivered me and also so grateful that I was a girl. Of course she'd known all along that I was going to be a girl.

"So there it was, the truth. I had been wanted, but only if I was to be a girl. But not in those last few weeks when, for whatever reason, she thought she might be carrying a boy. And I knew it. I felt it deep inside her belly and I knew I wasn't wanted.

"And now all these years later I still feel not good enough, not worthwhile, not wanted."

Had this child turned out to be a boy, he would most certainly have been emotionally abandoned, denied touch and love. Instead, when the mother discovered she had indeed gotten the girl she wanted, she showered love on her throughout her younger years, perhaps subconsciously in an attempt to make up for the impact of the fierce rejection she had directed at her those last few weeks. But the imprint was permanent, uneraseable, at least until, as a young adult, she uncovered it and we could begin to work it through.

All women have at least some curiosity about the child they are carrying. So what is the answer?

A need to know is a need to control, even if it takes the most basic form of preparing for the "known future." But that leaves one unprepared for the unknown future, which is vastly larger than the known. If the mother can truly detach from needing to know and live in God's will for her and her child, however that is expressed, she will not need to know the child's gender before birth. Gender will not even concern her. What would it matter? The child would be God's child, and she would be entrusted with carrying and caring for God's child.

Without that detachment from expectations, the mother carefully and subtly programs the child through the fetus to be, or not to be, the one she wants. She sets the environment around and within the child, for good or ill.

This power to set the environment is equally important even for those women who remain childless in their life. Whether or not a woman ever gives birth in the conventional sense, she continues to nurture all within her environment throughout her life. This impact is magnified from woman to woman. In a sense, the environment of the entire planet can be seen as an interlaced network of potentially nurturing environments.

Thus the harmony with which the new soul will walk its path – and its capacity for completing its destiny – is to a large degree determined in the womb.

Consider the impact on the soul and consciousness of the fetus if the mother spends her days quietly singing and relating to friendly people, versus spending them in argument and fear, surrounded by threat and rage.

The emotional attitude of the mother determines the development of the brain and the relationship of the brain to the body's neurology. The mother's traumas result in traumas to the fetus, akin in holes in the brain's neural patterning which can translate into major emotional problems later in life.

Do you not understand the impact of noise alone on the fetus? Play loud rock music and feel the fetus turn, trying to escape the assault. Play some beautiful meditative music or divine hymns and the fetus will be lulled to sleep.

Now examine what thought can do. One worry in the mother produces frantic neural signals throughout the body of the unborn child, constricting muscles, causing adrenaline flows and other glandular secretions. The fetus is assaulted directly and indirectly by all this activity.

To the unborn, everything that goes on in and around his mother is about him. Mother is angry – it must be about him. Mother is crying – what has he done? Before thought is formed, pre-thought reaction is there. As she thinks a thousand thoughts a moment, the fetus gets the message clearly, over and over and over again.

The young woman in her early thirties sitting across from me is in considerable discomfort. Her baby is threatening to be born too prematurely to be assured of a strong foothold in life. She is only six months pregnant and almost every hour she is feeling the initial signs of labor. The doctors have given her drugs, but they do not seem to be working.

I talk to her and her husband. They have come to me to receive healing energy because they thought it would help.

There are no guarantees, I tell them. The energy does whatever is necessary, and neither you nor I can tell what this child needs at this time. Perhaps he needs to be born and take his chances early with life.

She lies down on my table and I put my hands over her head. Within a few minutes, she had dozed off into a relaxed trance-like state.

I watch the movements of the fetus kicking inside her abdomen and see them gradually slow down and then grow quiet. I continue to transmit the energy to her, slowly moving my hands down her torso about ten inches above her body. When I get to the protruding abdomen, the warmth coming from my hands has become a bright sun shining into her.

Then I see and feel the child. He is turning toward the front where my hands are, his face up toward the warm light. He is beginning to smile. I never knew babies could smile inside. How beautiful!

For nearly ten minutes, I continue to beam energy to the baby and then I move my hands over her back – she is lying on her side – and, as I get to her lower back, I watch him turn again so he can continue to face the warm light. And then he too falls asleep.

For another half hour the three of us are locked into this trance-like state, the two of them in slumber and me captivated by the beauty I feel and see beneath my hands.

When I am finished, she awakes and tells me she feels relaxed. I do not hear from them again. Months later a mutual friend tells me that the mother was able to carry the baby well into the eighth month before delivery, without any further need for drugs. He was normal, healthy and came out smiling.

Producing peace in the environment of the mother, which is the environment of the child, made the critical difference. Rarely does it happen that quickly, but in this case the healing energies apparently released some critical fear or worry from within her that her child was trying to escape.

Next, consider the impact of environment when the child is born. According to ancient yogic energy science, the new baby has no aura of its own for the first 40 days. Imagine that! That is like living without a skin, just a bunch of raw, jangled nerves exposed to the elements.

Years ago, when I lived in New York City, I used to shudder when I saw brand new babies being carried by their unwitting parents on the New York subways. At first, the babies screamed, but in short order they grew quiet and had a kind of stoned look on their faces. The assault of sounds, blurred faces and bodies and speeding visions on platforms, along with smells, put them into a state of overwhelm.

In a similar fashion even a ride in the family auto can do much the same to a three-week-old infant. No wonder so many children are "fried," hyperactive, afflicted by nervous system disorders. While nutrition is an important contributor to such problems, these early nervous system woundings have a major impact.

During the first 40 days, for the sake of protection, the baby must be kept within nine feet of the mother all the time so that it is covered by the mother's aura. And her aura must be calm! That holds true day and night. The baby lives with her and sleeps between her and its father. Many extend this sleep practice as long as the baby is nursing. Certainly if parents wish to sleep apart from the child, the crib should be nearby in the same room.

The tradition in India, practiced also here in America, is that someone comes to live with the family for the first 40 days to take over the housework and meal preparation so the mother's full attention can be focused on the child.

For many people who practice this tradition, it has become a beautiful way of serving each other and an extension of natural at-home childbirth.

That is how life begins. Now let's look at how it all came about, or "how we are who we are."

3

HOW WE ARE WHO WE ARE

No woman really needs a man;
she has to be taught
to believe she does.

And then she's hooked.

How We Are Who We Are

Who is woman and who is man and how did we get that way?

When poet E. E. Cummings penned the words, "Candy is dandy but liquor is quicker," he was writing from a perspective and with a goal-orientation that could only be male.

Psychologists could examine these lines seven ways to Sunday and still miss that basic point. It was not written to put down women, to paint them as sex objects, to degrade their worth. It was written as a sheer statement of the male's dance of power and the role women play in that dance from the man's perspective. Failure to understand that basic need of each man for power has gotten many a woman in trouble – in trouble with the men in her life and with herself.

WE ARE NOT ALL THE SAME

The first thing to acknowledge is that men and women are not the same. Yes, we have similar urges and rat least some of the same equipment mentally and physically. But what is important, what comes first and foremost to a man or a woman is different.

Men seek power in all its forms, but most basically in money, position and sex. It is a goal-driven life.

Women seek love in all its forms, which includes acceptance, approval and friendship. To achieve this, women are eternally in process mode – processing this, that and everything that happens to themselves and to virtually everyone around them.

If we are different, then the next question that rises is, "Are we equal?" The answer to that is a resounding "No!" In fact, it's one of the silliest questions to arise in the classic, perennial tug of war between women and men.

All too much is made of the genders being equal in all sorts of social ways. Do you want to be equal with your neighbor? With your boss? Perhaps what we really want, is the equal right to be unequal on our own terms.

For a woman, equality would be ridiculous. Jean Paul Sartre once commented, "A woman who seeks to be equal with a man is lowering herself."

According to Yogi Bhajan, the old yogic texts tell us that women are sixteen times more powerful than men. Sixteen times! That isn't at all obvious, you say? Well, that's because you usually see that power on the negative side.

"Every time she says she's tired, I'm frightened, because I know she's not well, not really healthy."

The young man speaking to me is in love with a woman twice his age. The difference has really begun to worry him since she aged into her fifties and her health began to deteriorate.

"I want her to go to the health club three or four times a week and trim down, but she says she's just too busy at work. And the work she does is really important."

"Do you understand that if she takes time to work on herself that may mean there'll be less time for the two of you to spend together?" I ask.

"Yes, I do. But then she'll feel better, laugh more and we'll have more years together..." His voice trails off and he is lost in thought.

The woman is so powerful a force in his life that, in pulling herself down, she is pulling him down. Yet he would rather stay with her in a negative power state than leave.

The next day, I am talking to the woman in this partnership. She has come to me exhausted, and quickly succumbs to tears at the mention of her partner's concerns for her.

"Yes, yes, I know he's right. And I've watched his weight climb along with mine. I just can't seem to be able to change – my hours, my work habits, needing to eat to relax when I get home late. At least we get to eat together and then curl up on the couch. I won't give that up. What can I do?"

"You can start by changing what you do in the morning, not at the end of the day."

She looked at me startled. "That never occurred to me. But when? How? I usually get up just in time to dress and race out the door."

"Get up earlier."

She laughed. "With my late night work schedule? Fat chance."

"Right, a chance for fat to come off." I changed my approach. "You think you're a pretty powerful woman, don't you?"

She nodded her head yes.

"Then why not use that power for yourself? Command yourself to get up an hour earlier and go take a walk."

"It's too hot."

"Not at 6 a.m. Don't avoid the point. Are you powerful enough to give yourself that command, or does your alarm run your life?"

"What do you mean? Everybody gets up by an alarm."

"True, many do. They set it to wake themselves when they have to get up. You could be different. Some of us are. You could set yours to wake yourself an hour earlier when you want to get up."

"I won't want to get up at 6 a.m., believe me!"

"Perhaps not at first, but try it for awhile. Get up early and you'll be getting up by your choice, not just because you have to get up to get to your job."

"All this just to knock off a few pounds?"

"No. To show yourself how powerful you really are. You may just surprise yourself."

"Okay, I'll try it."

"No, don't try it. Life is trying enough. Just do it!"

I know she has to start making a positive difference in her life from the moment she gets up. Otherwise, no matter how strong -willed and good-hearted she is, she will take on too much baggage from other people – the real reason for her "weight" in this case – leave no time for herself and not be able to love herself. Eventually she will fail even her beloved partner.

This simple task is the first of several I will give her to help her get back in charge of her life. That is what drew her partner to her in the first place, her powerful take-charge personality. The hope that her positive power will return keeps him with her.

WOMAN'S POWER

No woman really needs a man; she has to be taught to believe she does. And then she's hooked

She is carefully trained from childhood to believe this, trained to believe she is helpless or weak or somehow lacking necessary ingredients for wholeness. She is trained by well-meaning parents and society-at-large to believe that she's needy, that she has to live as somebody's "other half" and not as a whole person.

Remember the song, "You're nobody 'til somebody loves you?" That belief structure, aimed solely at women, is as old as the hills.

The typical woman reared with this belief goes around thinking she has to find her white knight, her savior, her authority figure who will solve her problems and helps her make her decisions.

Of course she doesn't see the neediness in the man, and every man has needs. No man can survive happily without a woman, in fact, several women in many roles. Too soon the honeymoon between the sweethearts is over and she finds out that he doesn't have all her answers and that he's needy too.

For his part, he's equally taken in by the same lies. He finds her beautiful and a prize to be had, but then he finds she's needy – not a rock he can hold on to, but millions of grains of sand that want can pull him down. Try as hard as he can, he eventually feels strangled by her needy loving arms. Every time she complains, worries, cries and criticizes, she weakens herself in his eyes and in her own eyes and comes closer and closer to losing him.

Women, take hold of your power! Use it, and use it kindly. And know this: when you strengthen yourself, you strengthen him and everyone else around you too.

DO YOU DOUBT A WOMAN'S POWER?

Watch any woman and examine how she uses her power and how it affects everyone around her. So it was from the very beginning of each child's life.

Remember Mom? When she entered the room, wasn't there almost always a pause, a moment when Dad looked at her briefly, trying to read her thoughts to see if she was okay? And the kids also stopped to do the same thing. If it wasn't immediately obvious that she was upset, it seemed safe for everyone to resume what they were doing.

That's how powerful any woman can be, unfortunately in many cases in the negative.

You see, a woman may be sixteen times more powerful, but that doesn't necessarily translate into more powerful for the better. It can also give a woman the power to pull everything down around her with a mere frown.

To achieve that kind of power, man has to bluster and shout a lot and build a solid reputation for blustering.

Woman is the first power. According to old yogic beliefs, woman is the keeper of the emotional environment. God blessed her with all the elements in the universe so she could take care of the universe wherever she was – creating a universe of peace and harmony or a universe of discord.

Women are so lastingly powerful that a man will do and learn to do almost anything to keep a frown off her face, a tear off her cheek.

Her power is so impactful that it stops him in his forward motion to achieve and do something. It can also prompt him to remember flowers and theater tickets and other things he generally doesn't take time to think about, or plan to go on a cruise with her where most of the time he'll just sit around and read that action stuff he just loves!

When he tries to understand how she got depressed, he gets all flustered. Her power to pull herself down is so awesome and immense, it baffles him. She has pity pits and worry pits he cannot begin to imagine. Even if he tried to, he simply doesn't have the time and patience to do it.

He only knows that her tears or frowns can wreck his day. It's all he can do, under the best of circumstances, just to keep his day together.

Why should he hang in there with her? Because he has seen how her smiles and laughter can make his day, and how a few kind words from her can send him out the door feeling like a million!

He is capable of remembering that smile for quite a long time, or at least until her worries and criticisms reach some unbearable point. And then, all too often, some other woman's smiles and words break through and have their effect on him.

This is not to say that a man is fickle, only that he needs the positive power a woman has to offer on a daily basis. He needs her kindness, her heart.

Was it not a woman's face that "launched a thousand ships?" Was not the classic expression for the power behind the throne "cherchez la femme?"

That which is sought after always has more power than that which does the seeking. The quest itself would be nothing were there not some kind of Holy Grail.

All too often, however, in this century a woman's power is seen as defined by, and limited to, her sexuality.

Young girls have been programmed to "sell" their sexual attractiveness at a young age – witness the latest craze for the wearing of cosmetics among kindergarten-age girls. Seemingly at the opposite end, some social subcultures warn young girls that if they give away their virginity before marriage, no one will want them.

In other words, for both extremes, sex is seen as the young girl's power, her "hook," her weapon.

Certainly, denying sex to a partner has often been used by women as a punitive tool, however coquettishly that denial may be announced as a "headache" before bedtime.

The underlying problem is, in a largely male-driven society but where female neediness dictates certain values, women and men are given (and are giving each other) mixed signals. Some times they are depicted as having power, at other times no power.

Neither men nor women seem to be able to rely on themselves in this dance of power.

THE ROLE OF TEARS

Consider the role of tears. Do you know what happens when women cry? The conventional wisdom is that tears let off steam.

Well, ladies, that's nice psychology – if you believe you're a teapot. But tears actually wreak havoc in your energy fields, both internally and in your aura, your electro-magnetic field. Notice how exhausted you feel after crying. That's not relief, that's physical weakness. You've just depleted your own natural energy reservoir.

Will crying on your man's shoulder help to draw the man closer to you? For a short while, perhaps, the man will hold you, saying comforting words. All the while, he's trying to think what he can do to stop your crying because it hurts him so much to see you cry. And he has no idea what to do.

By instinct, the man knows you are more powerful than he is. Inwardly, he is angry at you because, ,with all that power you can't take care of yourself and you have to lean on him. Cry on him long enough and you'll find that he snaps at you more often.

And having cried and exhausted your auric field, you're even more vulnerable to his anger. You have holes he can zap!

Does this mean he isn't a "nice" person? Of course not. He's just seen so many whiney, wimpy women, beginning with Mom, who cried and argued and cried even more. He doesn't want a man-woman, but he does want a strong, self-reliant woman.

I've seen this over and over with clients.

"He used to enjoy coming home. We'd have dinner by candlelight and listen to our favorite music. Sometimes I'd have a problem and cry. He never used to mind my tears. Now he says he hates it when I cry, and I know he hates me."

The woman talking to me is a new client, a pretty brunette in her late thirties who is in the final stages of divorce for the third time. She has pushed away another man and doesn't realize how it happened.

"When did it start to turn sour?" I ask.

"About the fifth month after our marriage, he had started staying late at the office. Work just got busier. I was so lonely. And then I thought maybe he was playing around or something. I started to question him when he

came home and he'd get angry and then I'd cry and he'd hold me. It was all right then."

"But it didn't stop."

"No, it didn't. He kept working late. And then he forgot to call and tell me he was going to be late. I'd get angry at him when he came home. And then he just came home later, even after I was in bed asleep."

"And that's when you started to notice his drinking?"

"Yes, it was on his breath when he came to bed. I wasn't really asleep. Sometimes he'd roll me over and try to make love and I'd pretend I was too sleepy to wake up, and so he'd just roll back over and fall asleep. I was so afraid. My father used to drink and Mom would keep out of his way and play-sleep."

"Then what happened?"

"It deteriorated pretty quickly after that, but I never dreamed he would turn violent. He started living on his computer whenever he was home and I would go into his room and try to get him to talk to me. At first, he just ignored me. Then he started shouting. Then he threw something at me; I think it was a book. It hit my chin. I cried and he was shouting at me to get out."

The next day she moved out. Having beaten herself, she was finally beaten by him.

She wanted a cozy homebody; he wanted to go out and conquer his corner of the world. She felt insecure, doubted her own powers and turned the doubt on to him. Then she cried on him too many times until he began to believe she was messed up and not very powerful. And then he started to sulk and pull away.

Later, when I asked him what had happened, he simply said, "She changed. She wasn't the same woman I married."

But she was. She just hadn't shown him her doubts and fears, her lack of power. She started to treat him like a woman, showing him all those doubts and fears, the way women friends often share with each other.

That's a no-no. Never treat a man like a woman. They are quite different. They do not want to deep-process a woman's emotional garbage. Oh there are some exceptions, but in general most men want to see their woman as a gem, a winner, something other men will envy them for having at their side.

HOW IT ALL BEGAN

So, if men and women are so different, how did we get that way?

It all began in the womb after the soul designated which gender it chose this time around.

According to the ancient knowledge Yogi Bhajan teaches, during the final stages before birth, an acid wash passes through the brain of the fetus. In females, it appears to do nothing. In males, it numbs the right hemisphere. As a result, the male is more oriented toward left hemisphere activity.

So, men are more action oriented and have shorter processing-to-decision-making timeframes than women; as such, they also are more competitive and goal driven. Decisions must be logical.

Women, on the other hand, are intuitive, naturally long and thorough processors, so much so that they can have difficulty at times reaching conclusions, making decisions and taking action. Decisions have to "feel right."

Getting to a point where things feel right can take time for any woman. It is difficult to prove what is "right" to anyone else, especially a logic-driven man. That is why men forever complain about women's lack of logic. That is why they often jokingly allude to a woman's "sixth sense," her intuition, while at times acknowledging she has instinctively made the right choice.

Women are forever reviewing "first this side and then that side" and considering things from all perspectives. It makes women at times slow to act and extremely difficult for men to understand. That is because they are literally using both sides (both hemispheres) of the brain – nothing quick or simple about that.

Mistakenly, men believe – and women are told – that women think slower than men. Nothing could be further from the truth. The female mind is quick, able to range about and see so many details, side issues and matters of little consequence to her male counterpart. It is only the decision or choice-making output that tends to be slower.

Some proponents of pop-psychology believe that this long-processing tendency results from the female's desire to secure love and acceptance and that this motivation makes them timid to act and risk disapproval and rejection. But the true reason for this "slow to act" cycle is the two-hemisphere mental processing pattern.

Why would Nature, God or Divine Source have made a woman that way? Because she was responsible for carrying and protecting new life within her and those born from her. Her instincts were to assure the survival of the species.

She had to have two reasoning systems to rely on – logic and intuition. She was supposed to use either one, depending on the circumstances, and use the other as a crosscheck of her conclusion.

In a high-speed, goal and success-oriented world, however, this "advantage" can be a disadvantage.

Compared to her male counterpart, a woman's failure to find ready conclusions and make quick decisions can leave her seeking outside approval. On the contrary, her mind is generally quite quick but she is considering far more data than her male counterparts.

Help a woman speed up her decision making and you'll find she has a powerful mind!

A man will have made a decision and be halfway down the road while the woman is still processing the point. Days later she will bring up the matter again, introducing some new point she has uncovered, much to the disdain of the man who declares, "We decided that a long time ago!" and wonders why she is still considering it. While the woman may feel put down, nonetheless she will often have spotted several things he did not see that could cause problems along his path.

THE BASIC REASON FOR CONFLICT

Here lies the basic reason for conflict between men and women: each gender believes the other thinks and behaves (or *should* think and behave) like them. They act and interact based on that assumption. Remember the song in "My Fair Lady" called "A Hymn to Him?" The words start out, "Why can't a woman be more like a man?"

How shortsighted! How judgmental! And, if we were truly all alike, how boring!

"The wrong action is better than no action" - a popular Army slogan - could never have been coined by a woman.

"Look before you leap," would be closer to a woman's point of view. Or even better: "Fools rush in where angels fear to tread."

Notice how each statement is typical of the type of criticisms leveled by men and women against each other.

Men grow up at times browbeaten by Mom (later to be hen-pecked by wives) and criticized for their quick actions. Ask any man, it seems he can never do anything right for his woman.

Women grow up being told they are slow and therefore not good enough. So they experience perennial fears of rejection and abandonment and try to do anything to secure love. Ask any woman, it often seems she isn't bright enough, pretty enough, or something enough for her man.

The chances are, at least initially, that the mate doesn't really believe that about her. But if she buys his criticism of her, she subconsciously takes on that attitude as her own. Women can re-create Mom's or Dad's attitude about them in their mate. It's called negative conditioning.

So women never stop fighting those childhood battles, by trying to win over Mom or Dad in the roles of mates or would-be mates. They can divorce their mates but they cannot divorce themselves so easily from their parents whose influence and biases are deeply ingrained in their internal programs and belief structures.

Some men and women give up and try to think and act like their gender opposite. This isn't a logical decision at first, simply a desire to become the other parent and thus appear to win favor and escape the perceived criticism. It doesn't work, of course. What happens?

Women who take on male attitudes and speed up their processing often become known as competitive and heartless. Men who take on female processing roles and emotionality often slow down too much, fail to accomplish enough for themselves, and become couch potatoes. In both cases, the results can cause massive shifts in hormones and a genuine unhappiness.

Such role reversals, partial or near-total, can be devastating.

Notice what happens to a man who sits around all the time – overweight and depression. Notice what happens to a woman who sets out to win against all others – loneliness and depression. The only difference is that the breakdown happens faster with the man.

"Most of our time together I've been the bread-winner. He does some real estate investments, but my salary pays the bills. Mostly he just sits around and watches TV all day."

The woman talking to me came in for career counseling but is showing me quite a different face today. Lines of rage, disdain and criticism show on her face as she discusses her husband of four years.

"He's now more than 70 pounds overweight, and that doesn't help his heart condition. That's probably also why I'm having a weight problem now."

"Have you tried inspiring him in his investment work?" I ask.

Her answer tells me I was talking to deaf ears. "Of course. I tell him every day he should go to work, learn more about what he's doing so he won't make such bad decisions. His decisions are terrible, you know. I tell him every time about what pieces of property will sell and what won't sell, but he doesn't listen to me. He doesn't even talk to me any more about what he's doing, so I can't even give him the advice he needs to make good decisions."

Her face is growing quite red with the anger in her.

"Why not give him some space?" I say. "Let him fail if he has to, but let him work things out on his own."

"Why should I?" she counters. "He never leaves me alone. Picks on me. Claims I don't do enough around the house, that I'm sloppy and messy. How can I do it all? I'm just one person!"

Both people in this situation are probably re-enacting parent roles with each other. The man is more injured, since he has become virtually incapacitated, while the woman with her weapon-tongue is at least sufficiently able to continue to financially support them both. Both are miserable.

He is suffering from the male disease of inactivity. She is hardening with the female disease of doubt and negativity.

GENDER AND KARMA

All this doesn't mean that a woman can't employ logic in her thinking and that a man can't delve into right-brain work. It is simply a matter of where the balance lies.

The conventional belief is that each person has both male and female sides, just as their internal balance includes male and female hormones. So why should it matter if the balance goes too far off, if someone who is born female acts and thinks like a male, or vice versa?

The gender the soul selects in any given lifetime becomes the vehicle through which the soul can best work out its life lesson, its karma. If it chose female, the lesson is to be learned on female ground. The goal of each lifetime is to release karma, hopefully not build more. Of course, in reality, we create a whole lot more karma in each lifetime, which is why the ancients referred to "the wheel of karma," of birth and rebirth, as endless.

The only way off the wheel is to follow a destiny path, not karma, and then the karmic lessons burn off. That is a subject we will address later in this book.

Despite some beliefs, however, karma is no easier or more difficult for one gender than the other. Whatever degree of challenge our soul requires in this lifetime is exactly the degree of challenge we receive. Karma comes connected to whatever gender in which we chose to work it out.

If we came in as a woman, it is going to be easier and a more straight-through course of learning if we continue to play it out in female form and thought. For those few who prefer to go so far as to change their sex, surgically or hormonally, that too is part of their karma. However, if they do not live out their soul's original choice in gender, this will require the soul to return for other lifetimes to work that out.

Why? The answer is very simple. The most important factor in releasing karma and not building new karma is completion. Those things we do not complete in this lifetime will cause us to reincarnate again and again to complete. The point is: whether we came in this time as a woman or a man, we need to complete that choice and learn our lessons well. Now let's examine gender roles in light of our basic needs for sex, love and intimacy.

4

SEX, LOVE AND INTIMACY

Few women really want sex –
at least, not to the exclusive degree
that their male partners
generally do.

They offer it in the hope of
achieving intimacy and love.

Sex, Love and Intimacy

No three words in the English language are more misunderstood by both genders than sex, love and intimacy.

Let us start with the word that reflects the most primal need, sex.

Few women really want sex – at least, not to the exclusive degree that their male partners generally do. They offer it in the hope of achieving intimacy and love, and can come to enjoy sexual play when intimacy is abundant. Women who think sex is of primary importance to them have been carefully trained to believe it, just as they were trained to think they "need" a man.

For men, the situation is quite the opposite. Few men want love, at least not to the degree they perceive women need it. First and foremost on their minds is sex. That is not a putdown, simply a statement. They enjoy sex as a game. They want sex because it is a tool for power as well as a means of judging, from day to day, whether or not they have power.

So what happens when a woman, who really wants intimacy, not sex, sets out to pique a man's interest? She uses seductive behavior and language. Hours late, when she's gotten the man's interest and ended up in bed, she may feel she's been "taken advantage of" sexually, unaware that she "hooked" the man on his terms, not hers. She fed into his desire for a sexual playmate when she really wanted a friend and intimate.

That is why I often tell women to stop talking and acting like hookers. They want to hook a man into saying, "I love you." They dress for seduction; they talk the language of seduction, all for those three words. When he finally does say them, they "fall in love." That's quite an expression. With that one phrase, they have hooked themselves.

Do you not wonder why there is no expression "to rise in love?" Just about everybody falls in love. Think of when it last happened to you. How euphoric! And what did you do after you fell in love? You suspended almost all further evaluation of that person.

You gave away your heart, your seat of power, and to someone who most likely didn't want it in the first place and has very little idea of what to do with it.

If you had simply given from your heart and kept the heart itself under your own control, you would not have gone out of control and fallen in love, away from your critical faculties.

Now with your heart in someone else's hands, you have an excuse for acting uncontrollably, for being "madly in love" and not able to act rationally. And when he leaves you – and he most likely will – you will be crushed, because your heart will be missing. You'll hurt deeply because you won't know how to get it back.

Why did you give it away in the first place? Because you hoped it would be an exchange – your heart for his heart. But he wasn't out to bargain. He didn't want your heart, at least not at first. He probably wasn't in touch with his own heart enough to realize that his heart was what you wanted.

He knew you wanted to hear the words, "I love you," and so that was what he gave you.

Wasn't that great? Well, yes, at first you felt great. Then, later on, you became frustrated. You wanted more words from him, words from his heart. But the man's source of "I love you" was his mind, not his heart. When a man says, "I love you" it really means he's trying to love you. He has very little to say after that. In fact, it took a lot to get him to vocalize that much.

You must understand the nature of the man's vocabulary.

MEN OF FEW WORDS

Of all the straight talk Yogi Bhajan has given us about the games men and women play, this little piece of information amazed me. It was so true, by my own observation.

Just about any woman has twice the capacity for vocabulary as a man on any given day. When he goes for long minutes of time not talking, you think it's because he's holding back from interacting with you, preferring to watch the tube or read the paper, or just doze in bed. You complain that he has trouble communicating and therefore is insensitive.

Nothing could be more untrue. A man can be very sensitive but he doesn't communicate feelings as easily as you do. The man can communicate, but not in volume. Also, his thinking button – his word and thought-generating ability – gets turned off frequently, whereas yours is rarely turned off.

There are times you fear his silences and ask, "Honey, what are you thinking?" Either he tells you "Nothing!" or, if he has come to understand you a little, he tells you some vague fiction to quiet your disbelief that he could be thinking nothing.

That happens a lot after sexual intercourse when the woman wants to hear her man say something to confirm he had a good experience with her. She doesn't realize that her man, without a thought, just wants to sleep.

Actually, if there is one thing both the man and woman have in common, it is what they both want when they use the words "I love you." They both want someone they can trust. So in saying, "I love you," they are both hoping they have found someone they can trust.

For the woman, that desire happens much earlier than for the man.

This drives women from one sexual encounter to another, looking for the sensitive, communicative, trustworthy man, that "soul mate" who more often than not is a karmic link from lifetimes past.

WOMEN AND SEX

If women truly understood the role sexuality plays within a man, they would never give themselves sexually in the hope of achieving love.

Sexual thoughts – fantasies – occur to a man far more frequently than women can imagine. In every relationship between a man and a woman – including friends, sisters, even a man's mother – there is never one in which the fantasy of what she might be like in bed does not occur to him at least once.

I remember one student of mine at a Womanheart Retreat who, after hearing this statement from me on several occasions, suddenly spoke up with a laugh. "I didn't believe that when you first told me," she said, watching as other women nodded their heads in agreement.

"Then just last week a male friend of mine – we've been real close friends for several years – totally shocked me. We've been platonic friends, nothing more. And then suddenly, when I was telling him I was planning on getting married, he laughed and said, 'Great, I'm happy for the bastard. Now maybe I can get it out of my head, this delightful thought I've had for so long of jumping your bones!' Boy, was I shocked when he said that."

Consider for a moment that perhaps there is no such thing as platonic friendship. Perhaps Plato was referring not to heterosexual companionship but to the love between young men in the gymnasium, a kind of love he found perfectly natural as a harmless way for young men to explore male sexuality. That type of arrangement limited their interest in women – limited it but did not entirely eliminate it.

This is not to say that men can't be friends with women. Of course they can be helpful and supportive friends. But don't be so naïve as to think that a man's drives and impulses still do not include sex as a means of power and control.

That naïveté is the reason that women may feel cheated in a relationship. They give themselves sexually and rarely achieve intimacy, let alone the love they seek.

I once advised a young client being drawn head-over-heels into a sexual relationship, "Develop a friendship first. From a friend you may sometimes get a lover. But from a lover you rarely get a friend." I explained to her that, when the "in love" stage passed, there might not be an underlying basis for friendship.

An old rule of thumb from our grandparents' generation was this: that which takes longer to build is usually more enduring. You can "fall in love" in a matter of minutes and just as quickly fall out of love. But love built over time is not so easily destroyed.

Despite the fact that men seem to want sex on the first date, they too also enjoy a longer courting time, though for different reasons than those of the love-seeking woman.

If man achieves sexual partnering too easily, he often feels cheated. Man is a hunter who enjoys the hunt. The harder the game is to capture, the more he respects it and prizes its final capture. If the woman is indeed a prize, she will not be captured easily, no matter how many men seek her.

Some men who are highly skilled at hunting women prey easily on them. The game falls so easily that they quickly abandon it and go on to the next hunt. It is the process that excites them, not really the prize.

Women are often portrayed as the true hunters, but consider this alternative profile. As is the case with the great apes, the female courts by "displaying" herself to the male to lure him to her.

Either way you accept the view of who hunts whom, this dance of courtship is all a game of control. Only the goals differ between the genders.

What goals? Sex for the man, love for the woman. Understand this:

> *Even in dreams the man has sex.*
>
> *Even while having sex, the woman dreams.*

Dreams of what? Of her perfect lover. Of her knight rescuer. She rarely dreams of sex. Even when she does, that dream of sex is loaded with visions of her dream-lover.

That is why it is said that a man marries a woman and hopes she will never change, while a woman marries a man and hopes she can change him. He has in one glimpse seen his dream in her and he looks no farther. She has seen in him the possible raw material of her dream.

MAKE LOVE AND WAR

The man's dream, which he saw at first glimpse in his "perfect woman," is many things to him – lover, playmate, virgin, harlot, co-adventurer (doesn't Indiana Jones always have a female partner?), as well as the classical mother and sister roles.

He may see her in many roles, and expect her to play them with him when he is ready. But his biggest nightmare is that she will somehow change and no longer be his perfect mate. That covers just about any change at any time.

If she were to change, that would mean he might have to do battle with a woman and he simply doesn't know how to do that. Men don't like arguments at home, because they can't fight without having to win. And if the woman gets crushed in the process, then they know they've lost, because they've lost her.

Simply put, men and women don't make war by the same rules.

Men will do battle to win the "prize," whatever it is, and in the process kill many enemy soldiers. That is "the price of war." But then there is an end to the war and they can go on to the next game.

Women can continue a battle forever. Have you not seen how long a woman can hold a grudge against someone? Years later, she will remember some slight against her. Men fear that memory, because she uses it to hammer them down, inch by inch. The dream woman can become the nightmare enemy who incessantly attacks him. This is the unseen enemy, the sneak attack, the hell lurking behind the face of a so-called friend. That is why men fear and cannot trust women.

Normally, men love to do battle, but only with men. They are prepared to fight any man, but not a woman. Their banner could well read "Make love and war" – one makes war with men and makes love with women; those are the rules.

It is with a passion that they pursue conquest, whether it be to win the sands of Iwo Jima or a place in a woman's bed. To men, it is all a game, which to many women appears silly. But to the man, the battleground is where he comes alive, where he knows himself and experiences his life-power.

For a woman, life without a man can be lonely but still a life with power. Women can live without men, or without being pursued incomplete without a man, that is often because she has been trained to live by men's rules, whether that training came at the hands of father or mother.

Centuries of women have been schooled in men's rules. Even now, when women have a large degree of freedom and equal opportunity in the West, they often are left not knowing what they want in life and so continue the old games of entrapping a lover-mate.

For a man, being without a woman is not so crushing as it is to be without a woman to pursue. For him, the battle for possession of the woman is the ultimate battle. It was men who named ships after women, mountains as "the Grand Tetons" and who built up a whole language of sexuality that women often have a hard time relating to.

One form of civilized battle is competition in business. Until the women's revolution, business was seen largely as male turf. Few women were seen as sufficient in stature to men to engage in competition.

Consider how men compete. Have you not noticed that, after heated competition, the men go off to a bar for a martini or a beer? They simply don't know how to do that with women without continuing the battle as a campaign to control her.

Women all too frequently make the mistake of trying to act like women and also like men and continually confuse men. Women send out mixed signals and change them frequently. What are the rules, the man asks? The woman who expects men to open doors for her, or buy her dinner, cannot expect the same men to treat her like "one of the boys." The rules, as he sees them, are totally different.

In fact, if you ask many men, they will tell you that they prefer doing business with men because "they generally know and play by the rules," whereas women don't appear to men to play by any rules other than their feelings which seem unpredictable.

That is why, traditionally, men preferred to relate to women at home and to men in business, not directly because they wanted to put women down but because it was easier for them to separate out their game strategies into two different environments.

This is not to dispute the fact that this separation was clearly unequal and did in fact result in classifying women as second-class citizens for centuries.

But why did the men do battle? For whom did they go out in search of fame and fortune? For themselves, yes, but also to show off to their woman, their perfect princess on a pedestal. To show them how great they are. They came home valiant with the prize, asking only to be honored and told they did well.

Modern-day man is no different in this regard from his knight-in-armor ancestor.

He wants power to gain praise and feel right with himself. He can get that from other men, but men value most the words of praise they receive from wife, mother, sister, lover.

And the reverse is equally true. Most men can stand the insults of other men, but the hurting words of women can demolish stealth attack of the unseen enemy – the woman who reminds him of his mistakes – can over time turn him into a raging, vengeful animal, slashing back at the very woman he once adored.

Man has one great gift: he can often drop an angry incident (the past) and go off to the bar and have a drink. Woman has one great flaw – she cannot. She lives with the past as a continual film running in the back rooms of her mind.

When the woman continually reminds him of his past it stops him from going forward, on to some future conquest. The game stops, becomes reality, and it is no longer fun. And when life is no longer fun for a man it is a source of frustration and anger.

The man lives in the future; the woman lives in the past. He wants things to be light and fun, not serious, and she is full of heavy thoughts and worries linked to past disappointments.

THE POWER TO INSPIRE

If men and women are to come together in harmony, they must both learn to live in the present. The woman must take the lead. She must drop the past and learn to engage impersonally in personal play. In this way, she will redirect the man's focus from the future to the present and reap rewards from both his spirit of fun and his power to achieve.

Yes, she must take the lead. Why? Because she has the power to contain him, just as she did in the womb. Yogi Bhajan often uses the metaphor that "woman" contains "man," just as "female" contains "male." Every man holds that experience of blissful containment in his memory.

Thus in life she has the power to inspire him and deliver him to his higher self, not through demand and direction but through example and inspiration.

Women must master one great skill – to act impersonally personal. Her conversations and actions with men should be personal but her mind-set impersonal, detached from outcomes and expectations which are always linked to past experiences and judgments.

"I tried to keep from letting it show, but I just couldn't."

The face in front of me is full of defeat and exasperation. She has just admitted to "losing it" with her husband of six years and is trying to figure out how she'll hold on to him in spite of the fact she believes he is having an office affair. She made the mistake of not just expressing her fear that something was happening; she went all the way and accused him of having an affair.

"What did you expect to gain by accusing him?" I ask.

"I guess I wanted him to admit it."

"And that would make you feel better, that your worst fears were confirmed?"

"Yes, in a sense I guess so. At least I'd know what I'm dealing with."

"You're dealing with a man and all men will always, always look at other women. It's part of the game. Now what you've done is given him an excuse to act out what he might not have acted out before."

"How come? I'd think he'd be less likely to do it now that he knows I suspect him."

"You have a son, yes?" She nods her head yes. "When was the last time you accused him of doing something and then you found he went out and did it? Most every time, right? The psychology is: well, if I'm going to be blamed for something I might as well do it. Underlying that is the thought, 'She thinks I'm bad, I guess maybe I really am.' See what I'm saying?"

Her head nodded again. "So what do I do now?"

"Work on relating to him impersonally. Don't buy into expectations. You expected that he'd fall victim to this other woman. That says more about how powerless and uninfluential you think you are in his life, than it says about how powerful you think he is to resist her. Pull yourself and your expectations out of your communications with him."

We worked on a game plan together and she took a series of actions.

First off, she took several actions that were openly supportive of him in his work and drew him out on work-related topics and showed an interest in his accomplishments.

Since she had become friendly with several people in his department, she extended that to the new woman, inviting her to lunch, and casually making friends. This wasn't a fishing expedition, but instead an opportunity to demonstrate how well the marriage was working and to inspire a potential poacher to look elsewhere.

Once when he mentioned to her something about the woman, she gave no visible reaction other than "That's nice," and passed on to another subject of more interest to him.

Over time, he would notice that both her interest and the inquisition had passed.

Most importantly, we worked on her sense of self-importance in her life and in her marriage. If she had a truly interesting life of her own, she would be even more attractive to him.

The kids call it "getting a life" and it doesn't happen overnight. But teaching a new form of impersonal personal communications started right off.

First rule: not everything that is said reflects on you or is about you, even when someone expresses anger in your direction. Often their communication is far more about them, where they're at and what happened to them earlier in their day.

> *"He'd come home and tell me how lousy he felt and I can't help thinking it's something I've done or haven't done," she would tell me frequently.*

> *How absurd. "Was he talking about you?"*

> *"No, but he was telling me."*

> *"Of course. He had to tell someone. Maybe he was telling you because he felt safe enough to tell you and thought you were strong enough to accept it and not blame him for feeling that way. Did you ever think about it that way?"*

> *"No. Do you think so?"*

> *"Yes. There's certainly some evidence to support that."*

Second rule: when conversing with a man, consider the effect of your communication on him; think of his needs even more importantly than your own. Listen to his language. Learn to speak in the words he uses so that he has the best chance to hear you.

> *"I've learned that when I really want to say something that I know has value to him, I'll wait and bide my time until I see he is relaxed and open. Then we really can have a good discussion."*

Third rule: let him speak first. Even invite him to speak. Remember, he has only half the verbal capacity in a day that you do.

> *"When I do that, he'll tell me what he thinks about something and then he'll ask me what I think and really listen to me."*

Fourth rule: don't talk in the middle of your process. It will only confuse him and he'll try to come up with a solution.

> *"I see what you mean. He used to think I was so indecisive. And I guess I sounded that way, telling him first one thing and then another as it occurred to me. Now he doesn't see all my internal stuff and he just sees how I go about accomplishing things."*
>
> *"And how do you feel about your own decisiveness?" I ask.*
>
> *"Frankly, I think I'm better at making decisions. I don't get stuck on everything it takes to get something done."*

Fifth rule: don't ever try to have the last word. He'll never forgive you. Men need to feel they have closure. If you have handled yourself well in the conversation, what should it matter what the last words are?

"That's still the hardest thing for me to do," she admits after several attempts over a number of weeks.

"What prompts you to keep on talking?" I ask.

"Well, it's just that I keep thinking there's one more point to make."

"That's because you're still talking from your process." I shifted gears a little. "Okay, you draw him out first, yes, and he starts to talk?" She nods her head affirmatively. "Before you begin this conversation, organize your points. Select just two or three and prioritize them. When he's talking, bring them out in conversation, not as a hard 'this-is-the-way-it-is' statement but as a suggestion, kind of like 'what-do-you-think-of-this?' Don't get attached to his accepting it."

I watch her squirm a little as I say that. "That's right. Don't mentally label your way as the 'right way.' Just make the suggestion and wait. He may not absorb it or factor it into his process for several hours, maybe not until the next day, or maybe not at all. And if he does, don't let your ego and pride get into it when he comes up with your suggestion as his own idea. Don't tell him, 'I said that yesterday.' That just knocks him down and creates arguments. And how original are your ideas anyway?

"The point is that you will get something of far more value then just the credit for the idea. You'll get a harmonious home, a man who trusts you and therefore a man you can trust will be there for you. Make sense?"

She tried it once, tentatively, and it worked. Each time after that it worked even better. Their relationship did indeed become more harmonious.

SAD PROGRAMMING

It is sad that our lives are filled with the other kind of programming – the tapes, the radio and TV shows, the newspapers, not to mention all the family and so-called "friends" who continually reinforce the hooker behavior in women in the belief that men have to be seduced into bed to achieve life companionship.

Is it any wonder that date rape is on the rise? Is it any wonder that the battle of the sexes has turned angry and murderous? Is it any wonder that women in business are experiencing many of the same health and stress problems of their male counterparts?

Virtually every little girl is reared with the belief that she is nothing if she doesn't attract a man. She longs to be intimate and settles for being touched. And because she is touched only for sex, she may well turn off her feelings and become desensitized, detached, disassociated from her body and locked in delusion.

In short, she becomes an ice goddess, the nymphet who digs sex but has little or no feeling connected to it, and so fails to feel connected with men. What are her inner thoughts?

I'm sitting across from a woman I've worked with as a client for over a year. She was sexually assaulted as a child and her ability to relate intimately to the opposite sex has been further impaired by a cloying, co-dependent family. She has never married and claims she has no feelings "one way or the other" about sex.

Today she has brought in a music tape with a song on it she wants me to listen to because she says it really "moves" her. It is a song by Heather Nova called "Walk this World" from her CD "Oyster." Two verses stood out most to her.

"I'm sucked in by the wonder and I'm fucked up by the lies,

And I dig a hole to climb in and I build some wings to fly,

And I think that I could love you 'cause you know how to be free.

I want you to come walk this world with me.

With the light in our eyes it's hard to see,

Holding on and on 'til we believe.

With the light in our eyes it's hard to see.

I'm not touched but I'm aching to be;

I want you to come; I want you to come;

I want you to come walk this world with me."

"I listen to it and I feel like someone in me is melting," she explains. "It seems to bring out a feminine aspect in me."

It is the longing to be touched, and someone has finally spoken for her inner voice. "Do you remember the doll dream you told me about a couple of months ago?" I asked.

"The one where my mother was fixing my hair and I was like a doll sitting in a chair, watching her do it and feeling nothing?"

"Yes. How do you think the doll felt inside?"

She shifted nervously in her seat. "I think she wanted to get away," she said softly.

"Or dig a hole to climb in?"

"Yes, that's what she did. Because there was no place to fly to, nowhere to go, to get away."

"But in that hole she built, could anyone reach her?"

"No. She didn't live in her body. She lived in her fantasy world and so she wouldn't ever need much. So if life didn't give her anything, it didn't matter."

I knew it was time to switch gears. "That was your mother's doll. What about you? What do you want from life?"

She looked startled for a moment. "What do you mean?"

"You're not a doll. You're a living, breathing person. You have a job. You go to work each day. You meet people and make friends. What do you want from life?"

"I don't know," she was almost in tears. "I'm afraid to ask, to say what I want..."

"And do you want to be touched?"

She looks down into her lap, nodding her head yes.

"Then you have to come out of your hole. You have to fly. To love yourself because you can be free..."

"But how?"

"Put aside the fantasies. Your mother died several years ago. Isn't it time now to put the doll aside?"

"But maybe that's all I am, a doll."

"Why do you think you had the dream? How could you have seen yourself as a doll if you weren't that doll anymore? You were outside looking at her, yes?"

"Yes..."

"But ...?"

"But I could still feel how she felt inside. I still felt trapped inside her."

"Of course you could. Because you had feelings even then, only you didn't feel them then, did you?"

"No."

"And now you do?" She nodded her head yes. "So now you can feel what that doll felt. That means you stayed alive through those awful experiences with your family, and now you can feel both inside the doll and outside her, right?"

"I guess so."

I resorted to an old process we hadn't ever used before.

"Close your eyes, lean back, go back to that dream world where you saw your mother and yourself as her doll. Now, think what she was thinking; hear what she was hearing; feel what she was feeling. Look at the doll's face in the mirror and feel yourself behind that face. Feel your mother pulling at your hair as she combed it and curled it. Now, reach out and touch that face. That's right, touch your chin."

Her hand automatically started to move up to her chin.

"Now see yourself applying makeup to that face, putting on lipstick the way you want to, eyeliner and mascara, just as you want to."

A small smile starts to crack across the mouth. "Mother always hated makeup."

"That's right. And you want to put it on, so go ahead. And when she puts the comb down, watch her turn away and then you can start to comb your hair any way you want to."

"I want to cut it."

"Fine. You can do that. In fact you can do anything with this face and this hair that you want to."

"She'll hate it," she says, with a broad grin on her face.

"And you'll love it." I wait a few seconds to watch her pleasure. "Now, have you finished changing your face the way you want it?"

"Yes, but I think she's coming back."

"Fine. Keep looking in the mirror and let me know when you see her in it."

"She's there. She's horrified at my face and my hair. She's screaming at me."

"Okay. Take that makeup tube and that lipstick, and start painting her face, the face you see in the mirror. Go on, you can do it."

"She's screaming at me to stop."

"Keep going. Change her anyway you want to."

"She's crying now. But I'm changing her."

"Good. Let me know when you're done."

"Okay. That's good enough."

"Do you like her face better?"

"Yes, actually, she looks funny. I mean, she looks ridiculous." Her words are barely audible through her laughter.

This was the first major step away from childhood for this woman. Did she eventually find a partner, marry a perfect partner? Not yet, as of this writing, but she now thinks herself worthwhile. Partnership may yet come. But if it doesn't, no matter. She is becoming whole for herself and that is the greatest gift. Too many people are looking for that perfect partner anyway.

THE "PERFECT PARTNER"

So you think you want to marry and you've found the perfect partner. In other words, you hope you've found someone you can trust. So the question arises: are *you* a "perfect partner?"

Whether or not you think you are - and 99% of women secretly believe something deep down inside them is not all right or good - *don't tell him* you're not perfect.

A "perfect partner" is made, not born. You have to show yourself worthy of trust over and over and over again before he will be convinced.

So keep your secrets to yourself. Telling him everything about your past - your affairs, your mistakes - might seem to you a way to see if he can love you "in spite of who you are and all you've been through." Or you may think that telling him your worries and problems day by day will give him some necessary deep insight into your soul.

Quite to the contrary. What will gradually happen is that you will weaken his "love" for you, his trust in you.

Do you really believe that love, once spoken, must continually prove itself to show it can't be broken? Don't be naïve. Like Chinese water torture, a drop of problems a day or several times a day will lead to pain and breakup.

How so? What happens?

Man relies on a woman for strength – an inner power to prevail through emotional, financial, mental problems, particularly his problems. He needs her to be steady no matter how stressed out and pushed he gets. He wants a steady woman, a rock.

Yes, *he needs her*. If, instead, you act needy, he has no recourse but to try to take action to help – he's a creature of action, remember? For the short term, that's okay with him. You can get away with needing his help. After all, he grew up with the male-knight-in-shining-armor image also.

If, however, you continually present him with an image of yourself not as a rock but as a pile of sand, he will feel he has to continually shore you up. His nervous system cannot handle that for long, so eventually he will freak out.

It is all a man can do to keep his own world together. By basic instinct he knows you are far more complex than he is, and that he doesn't stand a chance of keeping your world together. If you can't do that, he sure can't.

Love is re-earned every day the woman is steady and the man sees and enjoys it. That is how trust grows. That is how love grows.

Men don't have the answers for you, so look to your own resources. You want a shoulder to cry on? Cry on a woman, or a professional counselor. Better yet, cry in your closet. There's no one there to play out their own agenda on you or live to remind you of it later.

If you cry on a man's shoulder long enough, he'll come to the conclusion that he has a needy woman with problems. If he wasn't obviously needy before then, he will become needy and he'll resent you. Eventually, he'll bite back at you, hours or days after he gave you the comforting shoulder.

By pushing his fear buttons you destroy the very core of relationship. What is the point of being in relationship?

The point isn't to see how far you can push each other before you crack, because once cracked is forever cracked. The point of relationship is to see how strong you are, how like a rock you are.

HOPE AND THE POSSIBILITY OF INTIMACY

Woman lives forever with the hope of possible intimacy. Man lives forever with the hope of conquest.

The difference is that man without conquest will eventually die, figuratively and even literally. That is why a man without a woman must seek conquest through power of position or money.

On the other hand, woman without intimacy can continue to live on with the hope that it may exist sometime, somewhere. From that hope she can give intimacy to others while not ever receiving it herself. But somewhere inside her sits the child waiting for the hand of kindness it never received.

The legacy of declining intimacy, handed down from generation to generation of women, has left this current generation mortally wounded. I have seen it time and time again among my students and clients.

When I first met her as a client, I was introduced to her by her father who asked me only "to fix her" so she could come back to work with him. She had been handed from one therapist to another for several years, all of whom had muddled through her mind, made a little headway and then passed her on. She was like a hand-me-down, worn and tattered. But there was a fire in her eyes that attracted me.

I came to know her by many names, all the personas she had created throughout her childhood to try to cope with her world. As I came to know them – there were 36 in all – I saw how well hidden she had made herself. It took many months of working together before she trusted me enough to emerge from behind the other faces.

"I had a dream the other night," she started the session out, reading from her carefully written notes to me. "I was sitting in my living room looking out the window. I was sitting there naked, watching people pass by my window. But they didn't notice me. I stood up and walked over to the window, but still no one noticed me. I think there must have been something wrong with me. That was why they didn't notice me."

Without commenting, I asked her to go on.

"So I opened the door and stepped outside. Suddenly people saw me and they were very upset. They called a policeman and he came over to me and told me I shouldn't be naked outside, that I had to go back in my house. So I did.

"And then my husband came in and sat down to watch the TV and he didn't even say anything to me. It was like I wasn't there for him either. I was so scared. I thought maybe I was dreaming what it was like to be dead."

"Did you feel dead?" I asked.

"Yes, I had no feelings at all inside me. But I wanted to get out of that house. I wanted to talk to the people. I remember speaking out at them from behind the window but no one turned. I guess they couldn't hear me."

"And did you try to speak to your husband?"

"No. I tried before. He doesn't hear me when the TV is on. So I just go in the other room and read."

It was a dream, but it was in reality a film clip from her waking life, played over and over again.

Gradually I learned more and more about her childhood. She grew up abused and neglected, watching her mother slowly die after her father abandoned the family. She never forgave him for, in effect, killing her mother. Her wound, however, was even greater.

"I can't hug people," she said once, in a moment of insight. "I can barely stand it when they hug me. It makes me sick to my stomach."

That must have been the way she felt inside, when the child was being hugged by someone who would later throw her aside. They were all the same, huggers and abandoners.

Inside her was a seething river of rage and grief. It would only come out with strangers, or in our sessions. Then the emotional avalanche started to surface at her job. She could barely hold it in check and it frightened her.

But with this emotional upheaval, the last of the childhood "personas" disappeared into the fabric of her past and she began to emerge as a whole person demanding things for herself including friends, intimacy and, yes, even a husband.

It was not an easy coming-out party. She ran smack dab into a world of other demanding people who had little time for her. Some she handled swiftly and put out of her life, but the key relationships with mother and father had to be faced.

The first dream she shared with me in the beginning regarding her mother had a recurring theme: her mother always stole her car and wrecked it, leaving her unable to get away. Almost exactly a year to the day later, she was able to put her mother's control over her to rest. It came revealed again in a dream.

"I dreamed that my mother and I were driving to a meeting," she began. "It was some course we were both attending."

"Were you in the same car?" I asked.

"No. We were driving separate cars."

This was quite a shift. I was happy to hear it.

"We parked at the edge of a cliff overlooking the ocean far below. I remember her car was only one car away from the edge, while I parked mine further away than that. We went to the meeting. I had done my homework and she was surprised that I had. She even said to me, 'Why did you do that? It really wasn't necessary.' I felt she was putting me down like she always did.

"While we were at the course, I looked out the window and I saw the cliff start to crumble and the car in front of hers and then hers fell into the ocean. My car was all right; it was a little farther away.

"Later that night, I had the same dream, only I changed a few things. First off, I parked my car up on a hill much farther away from where she and the others parked by the cliff. And when she asked me about the homework, I just walked away without saying anything to her."

The next dream she had, she looked clearly into her mother's face when she questioned her about the homework and, for the first time, she saw the rage underneath the mask her mother wore – the rage directed at her. She did not respond, nor did she walk away.

In another dream, months later, she left her mother for the last time, watching her die and turning her back to the drama, walking out the door, leaving her whole family sitting by the bedside and starting out on her own life at last. Gone, without emotion, without even a wave goodbye.

The next time she saw me, she had made her first true adult friend at work. "I still feel like a weirdo," she laughed.

"But now you're not alone anymore," I added and she nodded her head. "At least one other person out there feels like you. You'll find others."

Others who will enjoy her, others she can invite into her living room, into her life. So she need never go naked and unnoticed again.

The drive to be intimate has gone so long unsatisfied, that young women are sacrificing themselves to at least be touched. It is the only piece of intimacy they can command, but the price is going naked, being handled and abandoned. They know no other way.

ACTS OF INTIMACY

We are taught to think in terms of acts of sex and acts of love. We all know what acts of sex are, and acts of love, yes? He brings you roses; he calls you to let you know he's thinking of you.

What is growing slimmer and slimmer in our society are acts of intimacy, events that build trust in us, that let us know it is safe to come out from behind our walls, and safe to let someone else in. Being intimate all too often means living on treacherous ground.

So what is the first act of intimacy that a baby requires and recognizes? Not touch, not words - important as they both are. The baby cries and Mother comes. Someone hears him but, more importantly, _someone is listening_. That is the first intimate communication - listening. And the baby soon comes to learn the difference between "someone is there" and "someone is listening."

Being listened to means our needs are being met and we are somebody special. Not being listened to, over time, means we may not survive; we may have to fight to survive, because no one is there to meet our needs when we are helpless.

Beyond listening, acts of intimacy include gentle touch, soothing sounds of voice, pleasant taste and aromas. These are all means by which baby learns to trust the world. The world first smells like mother and tastes like her. It sounds like her breathing and her gentle voice. She creates the total intimate environment, the first experience of trust.

If we are lucky enough to experience these harmonious intimate communications after birth (even before birth as we resonate with Mother in the womb!), then we have a pretty fair template against which to match experiences with others, to see if they add up to some semblance of a trustworthy intimate partner. If we don't experience this early, we have little or no way of knowing what and who to trust.

To the adult, acts of sex without acts of intimacy are meaningless, and acts of love are hollow and never fully trustworthy.

5

DR. JEKYLL & MR. HYDE
VS.
THE 30 FACES OF EVE

The dumbest man
knows by instinct
how much more powerful
you are than he is,
and it's unnerving to him to see you cry.

Dr. Jekyll & Mr. Hyde
vs.
the 30 Faces of Eve

To understand further who we are as men and women, we must understand our cycles.

Conventional wisdom has it that women have cycles and men do not - though many have long suspected that men do. The reality of male "change of life" - called andropause - is now well accepted throughout Europe. It occurs earlier than menopause does for women, at age 36. If not at that time, certainly by 40 every man feels he is "getting old." It is a crisis for a man that few women can appreciate, simply because women have crises on a frequent basis about "growing old" and are therefore more used to them.

Cycles for women are thought to be exclusively linked to the menstrual cycle and this accounts for their observed instability, including fluctuations attributed to PMS.

Now let us put this belief aside and go into a deeper understanding based on yogic knowledge thousands of years old taught by Yogi Bhajan.

It is not that the descriptions here are wrong, only that they are shallow and inadequate for deeper understanding.

A MAN'S BASIC CYCLES

The man actually has an ongoing cycle; it is called the 30-70 cycle." It has a shift every seven days. One week the man appears strong and in charge of his world. He's on top of everything and running at 70% or better. The next week he is unsure, seeking support, and cranky and angry if it is not there for him. He's running at only 30%, sometimes less.

The week doesn't shift with the calendar week. Each man has his own shift point. It may be Monday night, or Wednesday morning.

I've observed that the shift point is hard on a man. It may be a sudden jolt, an unexplained downer, or on the up side, suddenly an unexplained elation and a mad dash back to work. Once he's past the shift point a day or so, he perceives he's back on an even keel. Actually his percentage points can start to improve also.

Our male friends are probably balking at this point. They like to think of themselves as operating more consistently and vacillating over a smaller range, somewhere between 70% and 95%. Many do not observe themselves critically. They are, after all, rapidly in motion, goal directed and going for the gold!

Men have also learned to cover up their weaker moments, so well so that, not only do they fool you, they often fool themselves into thinking they do not have highs and lows on any regular basis.

Have you ever seen the face of a little boy trying to look like a "big man?" Any mother has. Now apply that observation to a grown man and learn to spot when the face of the "little boy" is hiding behind the tough exterior of the big man. He will talk and posture like he's big, but the pout and worry are still there on the face underneath, asking for the woman's support. He may just want to cuddle, or take time off and go for a ride. All doers on the run must have time off. You would ask it for yourself. Why not allow it for him?

There is a special challenge in dealing with him in these cycles.

If you act like some mothers do and tell him to be responsible and take charge of things while he's in the 30% cycle, he will feel hurt and unsupported and remember you weren't there for him. It may be only a little hurt at first but if that mismatch between the two of you continues, it will build into a major "I can't trust her to be there for me" hurt.

Exactly seven days later he will shift into the other gear. If in the 70% cycle you treat him like a little boy, telling him how to do things and talking down to him, he will feel insulted and he will remember that too.

If the woman in the man's life doesn't understand these cycles and sees them as random shifts with no predictability, he will appear to her as either Dr. Jekyll or Mr. Hyde. One she loves and the one she fears, lurking behind the corner to jump out at some unpredictable time.

Accept this fact: when he is enraged in his 30% mode, he can be a fearsome thing. He feels the lack of power and he has to seek power in some form. You may not understand it, but please accept it. He may use food or alcohol, or the most primal form of power to a man, sex. He will demand sexual attention at that time, yours or someone else's if you are not emotionally available.

THE ROGUE CYCLE WALKABOUT

In addition to this weekly cycle, he has another one that hits at rare and unpredictable times. It is called the rogue cycle.

For the longest time, a man will be steady in relationship to you, the woman in his life. He will be absolutely loyal and dependable. Then, all at once, the rogue cycle hits. He will go veering out into space, so to speak.

It may even look to you like a straight line away from you, but actually in most cases he will eventually come back. Think of it as the rogue wave in the ocean in a fierce storm, that one wave that comes every 20 waves or so that is much higher and hits harder against the boat.

The aborigines call this occurrence in men a "walkabout." It may be a sign a boy is coming of age, or simply something a man has to do from time to time.

To Western urban dwellers, it may look like a man's sudden desire to go on an extended fishing trip alone or with "the boys." When a man is somehow inhibited from doing this, he loses something of his power and identity.

This is no reflection on the woman. It is nothing you have done, no inadequacy on your part, and certainly no rejection of you. You should not assume that this is some new norm for him. It is a fluctuation, a time when a man should be left to do what he wants, to go forage in his wilderness until it's his time to come back. There is no special activity the man engages in - not some sexual encounter, as much as you may fear that. In some way or other, he just has to leave and "do his thing."

The rogue cycle may not occur for years. When it does, it may last only for a few days, or a week or two.

But he will come back. He will quickly forget what has happened and expect his world to still be there, the same as when he left it.

What happened when he left may have shattered the woman's world - a jolt that sent her into a frenzy of self-analysis, low esteem and depression, followed by accusation when he returns.

You must stay steady. Don't beat him up verbally and accuse him of all sorts of undependable behavior. If you do stay steady, the chances are good that he will come back soon and stay happily by your side.

"How dare he be allowed this!" you may say. "Why doesn't he just grow up?" Well, when he's together, he tolerates a lot from you, a lot that confuses him. Think how emotionally unpredictable you can be, and forgive him for his occasional weirdness.

Surely you can take some comfort from knowing he is also a creature of cycles, as you are. Surely you can understand that – as freaky and flaky as you are in your menses – he is that way often, in a constant battle to keep his world going.

Forgive him, but do not forget. Remember that the rogue cycle will occasionally come. Remember that the 70% week is always followed by the 30% week. Be prepared with your own emotional steadiness.

It is only his shifts that frighten you. You were not prepared. Most likely you were engaged in your internal dialog with yourself, focusing on your problems and the events that still were pressing in on you for decisions. You did not see the early warning signs he was putting out. Then suddenly he startled you. You peeked outside yourself and looked at him and he seemed like a stranger. He had already changed and you were not able to handle it.

There need be no reason for fear if you stay alert. Observe the present cycle and prepare for the shift. The man has only these two faces, while you ladies have countless faces, appearing to change from moment to moment.

To the man you often appear as the "30 faces of Eve," an exaggeration of the classic film on female schizophrenia. Think about how often your mind shifts gears. Every time it does, your face changes. And the man has only what he sees on your face to go by, to judge your mood and how approachable you are.

He knows how quickly he can change and he needs you to be stable. It is all he can do to handle himself. He cannot take care of you, too, at least not for very long.

The menstrual cycle is in part responsible, but more fundamental is the fact that we women are creatures of our metabolism. If our colon goes off, if we can't digest and eliminate easily, we go off. It's that simple.

I've observed the truth in this teaching of Yogi Bhajan's over many years working as a counselor and healer.

When women are cranky, fearful, argumentative, whatever negative emotion, it's the result of metabolic shifts caused by our thoughtless intake of foods that hamper and harm us. Most of our psychological problems are not the result of things that occurred outside us, or that occurred 10, 20, or 30 years ago. They're caused by today's caffeine and sugar, following a lifetime habit of caffeine and sugar, eating too late before going to bed, and a host of other poor dietary habits.

Now, I don't mean that the internal programs established in us by our parents and others in our formative years aren't problems. Of course they are. But what kicks them off over and over? We dump on ourselves physically and the stresses on our body provoke states of fear and worry, trigger old patterns and an instant shift in mental gears.

Then there's the case of tears. Do you think you cry because you have problems? You cry because your glands are backed up and can't efficiently process your wastes. Sure, there's an emotional cause that the mind knows, but sometimes (have you noticed?) you can handle a big issue and other times you can't handle the littlest one. Wonder why? Your diet has overloaded your glands and they can't take the pressure.

Man doesn't really understand this. He sees it as another facet of your unpredictability and he has a hard time coping with it. You say you just want to put your head on his shoulder and cry. That's okay from time to time, but understand this: it really rattles him.

You see, the dumbest man knows by instinct how much more powerful you are than he is, and it's unnerving to him to see you cry. It's even more worrisome to him to see you ill. It can shatter his world, just the thought that something might happen to you and you won't be there for him.

But he can tolerate illness, even extended illness, if you are emotionally calm. Show your tears to a woman friend, or cry in the privacy of your closet. A man who senses you're weak will resent it and over time pick arguments with you and tear you down.

He wants and requires an emotionally steady woman, a rock in the sea of storms through which he makes his way. That is why he comes home to you day after day.

Have you ever noticed how sometimes the best looking guy stays loyally married to a rather homely woman? Ask yourself, what has she got? She has an emotional steadiness he has come to depend on and admire. He is proud of her for that and will brag about it to his male friends.

Now ask yourself, how mentally stable are you? Can you count on yourself from moment to moment, or rather, can you count on your moodiness coming up? By comparison, men, with only two faces, are far more stable than you with your many faces.

Control the metabolic shifts and you control your mind and your moods. Eat right at the right times, exercise and rest in the proper amounts at the right times, and life will be much sweeter.

This is how your steadiness is built, not just for your man's benefit, but most importantly for your benefit.

A WOMAN'S MOON CENTERS

Before we proceed further, it is important to examine a woman's basic cycles.

Most women understand that their emotionality is ruled to a large degree by their reproductive cycle. Yogi Bhajan has spoken often of this, giving us far deeper insights into the shifts in our menstrual or moon cycle than a Western approach can reveal.

A man has only one moon center, the chin, which is covered by hair to keep him emotionally steady. A woman also has a moon center on the chin but no hair to provide steadiness. In addition to this sensitive area, she has 10 other moon centers. During her 28-day cycle, every 2½ days her moon energy shifts and at each site she is emotionally quite different. So she fluctuates far more frequently than a man. These centers are called the "11 limbs of the woman."

If a woman is meditative, she can develop the sensitivity to spot the shift from one center to the next. In learning to do this, she can prepare in advance for her mood change and compensate for it in her regular program of meditation.

Now here are the centers and how you can spot them:

- When the moon energy is in her hairline (the arc line or halo), she is clear, intuitive, very conscious. Nothing can move her an inch.
- When the energy is in her cheeks, she is almost explosively out of control.
- When it is in her lips, she will talk about anything.

- When the energy sits in the sunspot on her ear lobes, she will be prompted to talk about values and God until all hours of the morning.

- When the energy is in her eyebrows, she is full of fantasy and imagination, building sand castles.

- When it is in the back of her neck, she is very romantic and even a tiny gift of flowers will make her go nuts.

- When the energy is in her breasts, she is compassionate and giving, even foolishly.

- When the energy is in her navel, she is most insecure, particularly about recently made decisions.

- When it is in her inner thighs, she allows no one to contradict her. Her way is the correct way.

- When it is in her clitoris, she wants to socialize, meet new people, and is very charming.

- When it is in the membrane of her vagina, she also wants to socialize.

A woman's natal moon center chart will not shift, except in some situation of real trauma.

Following menopause a woman becomes more steady, like a man, and she must learn to adjust to this change.

Speaking as one who has long passed menopause, I can attest to the fact that, if you are a regular meditator, this period of your life can be a most happy one!

It is important for each woman to learn her own cycle. Through meditation you can develop the ability to sense your shifts.

Understand this: in a world where women must relate to men in many roles, this emotional fluctuation every woman goes through can be unnerving to the men close to her. It can provoke frustration, ridicule about PMS, even rage.

The more she can be aware of and in charge of her own mood shifts, the stronger she is in herself and the more powerful she is in relationships where her steadiness is all important.

Now let's look again at the man and not shirk seeing him at his worst.

THE FACE OF RAGE

Sometimes a man has to deal with a woman at her worst. Her dark side is doubt and fear, and she can hold on to those fears with considerable tenacity.

The dark side of the man is rage. Every woman knows it and fears it. It is often viewed as the face of the abuser, but it is more basic than that.

For a man, rage is essentially power turned inward, inherently self-destructive. If his woman gets in the way, naively thinking she is somehow involved or trying to stop it by direct intervention, the rage can turn outward against her.

How destructive is this rage? More than you can imagine. I remember Yogi Bhajan describing it in this simple picture:

A male gorilla enraged will beat his chest brutally in a display of his power. In fact, he is the only animal that will become so enraged and beat his chest so hard and long that he will tear flesh, break bones and bring about his own death.

That is the face of rage. That is the same face of enraged man as instinct-driven animal. Any threat to his power can ignite that face - a perceived rival, a sexual denial from his mate, the withdrawal of power substances such as alcohol or drugs. Whether or not that threat is real in fact, it is real to him.

In that rage he is very dangerous, both to others and to himself.

Other animals have a cut-off valve. Like the big cats and their household-size cousins who will engage in confrontation and then suddenly turn and lick themselves in the familiar displacement activity that breaks the emotional state. This keeps them from short-circuiting their brains with their own build up of neural tension.

But not the male primate, be he gorilla or human. When he is enraged, your best response is to stay clear of him, avoid eye contact which can be viewed as confrontational and agree with him. Then, when you can, serve him some light snack or food that, once eaten, will gradually simmer him down.

Now I know that no man is truly a wild animal – at least not when he is in control of his own mind and not on addictive substances. Yet each woman has to understand that this potential underlies a man's anger tantrums. She has no power sufficient to confront it. She should not even try.

If you try to confront an angry man, you will get run over, no matter how powerful you are or think you are. Women are simply not able to muster enough direct energy to equal that of the man. You might as well try to stop a stampeding herd of cattle by standing in front of them.

Yes, there are some exceptionally powerful women, and some weak men, but don't be fooled by the exceptions.

THE FACE OF MOM

So what face does the man see on you? What face does he want to see?

That depends on what face he saw on Mom. Based on earliest experiences, a young man makes one basic decision about his future mate: either he wants a girl "just like the girl who married dear ol' Dad" or he wants the exact opposite.

It was what he saw on Mom's face that made the critical difference. Either it was a face he could please, that humored his weaknesses and rewarded his "wins," or it was a face that appeared critical of him at every turn of the way, a face and voice most likely equally critical of dear ol' Dad.

How could mothers be so different?

It all depended on how she coped with the Jekyll and Hyde in the little boy. Ever hear the expression that says every boy has a "little devil" in him? Most folks see it as a joke. It most likely came from some mother who had had enough of her boy's sloppiness and dirty clothes dropped everywhere, his pranks, and his fistfights – especially if she was carrying the work all alone or with little support.

If women don't understand men, often they do not understand little boys. That's why dads are supposed to be there, to help Mom and balance things out for the guy.

How many families today have both parents equally parenting the kids? Fewer and fewer. The TV tube was the primary parent for most of the last generation, and the computer video game is taking over with this one.

If Mom got cranky when her boy brought home a lizard and gave it to her, she didn't even remember her words of rebuke. For her, it was over with quickly. But he was deeply hurt.

Have you never seen your pet cat capture a little bird and bring it to your feet? It's a gift for you. Don't scold the cat. Don't scold the boy. It's their way of showing they're thinking about you, their way of showing love.

When a young boy comes home all tattered and dirty, first ask him how his day went and praise him for the battles he fought and won. Then you can take him and his offending clothes to the laundry room.

Being clean is irrelevant to most boys – girls yes, boys no. Most little girls want to look pretty and please everyone. Boys want adventure to please themselves and have tall tales to tell.

Yes, you can train him to take his dirty clothes into the laundry room, or at least to stop throwing them on the floor (maybe put them on the floor of the closet.) Some boys respond faster than others.

But if you try to train the boy out of him, you get a hurt, eventually angry teenager. He may cut you off, cease to hear you, hang out only with friends and come home too late to interact with you.

This situation can also distance him from his father, since he may view him as your accomplice directly, or indirectly, if Dad simply avoids interfering on his behalf.

You see, little boys take comments as criticisms. They don't want to displease. Most often, they're so involved in whatever they're doing, they just don't think about anything else.

In fact, they can't stand it when Dad does something that displeases you. They are even more horrified when something they do, usually in all innocence, displeases you. Don't let a casual comment from you become a pattern – and for boys a "pattern" is set much quicker than for girls, who can offset a perceived negative situation with a special hopeful outlook.

Once a pattern is set, the young boy believes that he displeases Mom and she will make a federal case out of almost anything he does. In fact, if he believes her response, everything he does is wrong.

"You're a bad boy!" should never be said. That phrase alone creates bad boys. They leave home, hit the streets for adventure and, these days, are on the fast road to prison or an early death.

Behavior can be labeled bad and pointed out. Boys are not bad, unless told so often enough.

So should mothers coddle young boys, overlook their bad behavior and mistakes? Of course not. They should be corrected. But first, enjoy your sons and ask them to share their little adventures.

Remember it is through adventure that boys shape their male identity. They are not driven by the need for relationships as girls are. However, if they fail to please the first woman in their life, Mom, they will have great difficulty in creating a happy relationship later with a wife.

So important is that first woman in their lives, it will shape their relationship with everyone else they meet who is in a male-female relationship.

For instance, if Mom is abused, verbally or otherwise, and her son is too young to defend her, he will take an instant dislike to any man he may meet throughout his life who looks or talks loudly like Dad.

"I hate him for what he's doing to you! He's pushing you around just like Dad pushed Mom around."

I am witnessing a session between a grown brother and sister. She has asked me to mediate because he is interfering in her new marriage.

The brother, Jack, is in his forties, twice married and divorced, and quite honestly trying to look out for his kid sister Jenny who, in her thirties, is attempting her first marriage. The problem is, Jack believes Jenny's husband is a woman abuser just like their father.

"I waited this long just to be sure I wasn't going to marry someone like Dad," she responds. "I don't want to live a life like Mom. You should know me well enough to know that!"

"But he's loud and he embarrasses you with other people."

"Sometimes."

"Like when he blew up all over that woman at the dinner party. That was just like Dad."

"No it wasn't. He was provoked. That woman butted into something that wasn't any part of her business. It was a misunderstanding between Dan and another woman, and she butted in loudly. She'd had a couple of drinks."

"Don't make apologies for him."

"I don't. I love him."

"Yeah, that's what Mom said too."

"Well, he could have controlled himself. It wouldn't have hurt him to have a little restraint."

She is silent for a moment, her eyes lowered.

"So your husband is a little combustible?" I ask her, shifting the focus a bit.

"He probably shouts at her at home, too," the brother shoots back.

I turn quickly to the brother. "Have you seen them like that at home?"

"Well, not exactly. But he talks loudly to her, orders her around."

"Jenny, does he order you around?" I ask her.

"No, but he is bossy sometimes. He's really protective of me and wants the best for me. Sometimes he's overly strong about it."

"Pushy, I'd say," Jack shoots back.

I look at him sternly. "So you see similarities between her husband and your Dad?"

"Damn straight I do. Not just similarities. He's Dad all over again!"

"And what do you see, Jenny?"

She pushed a tear off her cheek. "I see a world of difference. He may be at times a little loud and bossy, and socially irritable, but it doesn't come from anger and disgust with people like it did with Dad. It comes from anxiety about being around people. He gets edgy. Normally he avoids being in groups of strangers, even in groups of more than two or three friends. And with me, no one could be further from Dad. He's the most protective, loving man I've ever known."

"So this isn't a parallel situation?" I ask. She nods her head in agreement with me. "Not even a similar situation?" She nods again.

I turn to Jack, whose face registers disbelief. "Well, Jack, I guess you have to drop the 'ugly Dad' template."

"What do you mean?"

"You have to stop holding every man up to the picture of your Dad and looking for similarities. Finding one or two doesn't mean you have a parallel situation. Then you think you see similarities with the woman, and

none may exist. You couldn't rescue your mother then, and you can't rescue her now."

"I just want to see women happy," he spoke quietly now. "And if I can help..." His voice trailed off.

I smiled at him. "You can help by backing off and trying to see the whole situation. And if you want to get involved, ask permission first."

Some day, Jack may marry happily. First, he will have to stop trying to rescue the women he dates and let them grow their own way.

It is a wonderful goal for a man to want to please a woman. But he may not know exactly what will please her. Sooner rather than later, he has to learn how to also please himself, how to live a life where making others better is not the main focus of his life.

THE FACE OF TRUST

As the young boy grew, he kept trying to become more and more powerful so some special woman would trust him. He is looking for a face of trust. Can you give it to him?

Why do you think a man seeks power in business, money and all those possessions? So someone will praise him, confirm to him he's powerful enough to be trusted. He doesn't totally know how trustworthy he is until others tell him, and there is no one more important in that than the woman he chose.

But, you say, what woman can trust a man not to make mistakes? Well, can you trust yourself not to make mistakes? And is a mistake so bad? How else do we learn? Nothing is a mistake if you learn and grow from it.

What do you really want from him?

Perhaps you want someone who makes no mistakes so you can be covered, you can be free to make your own mistakes. How unfair! How unkind!

Forgive and accept your own mistakes and do the same with his. Reclassify them. Call them hurdles, or learning experiences, or some other term.

See his mistakes, but then chose to overlook them.

If you want to change him, do not use words as your weapons. Use a smile, a hand on the shoulder and perhaps some special food he likes – something little, not a banquet. Wouldn't you want the same, some quiet support when you feel you goofed?

Men need to see a smiling face, consistently. That is a face to be trusted. Can you be such a face?

We women often forget to give a smile to ourselves. We get locked into our downers, our depressions, and men are so frustrated because they feel they have to do something – anything – to get us out of it. It hurts them to see us down. But try as hard as they can, we won't budge until we're ready. They instinctively know we want them to cover us, but they don't know how to pull us out from depression and doubt.

No man can travel inward and down half as far as we women do. We got ourselves in, and it's up to us to get ourselves out and never go back down again.

Instead, many women criticize their men not only for what they do, citing their mistakes or telling them they're not good enough, but also for what they don't do.

Women are the creators of the environment. It can be an environment of peace, or one of doubt and distrust. The first will inspire man to become devoted and noble. The second will lead to his rage and downfall. Which do you want? It's up to you.

Each man wants a home that is safe for him, safe from the arguments and the war zone of his day. That's what they mean by their castle, their refuge.

"You mean, he doesn't want me to argue with him?"

The face behind that question, delivered with an incredulous look, is that of a woman in one of my Womanheart retreats. She has just realized that her husband does not want her to confront him and argue back at him. It was quite a shock.

"No, he doesn't," I answer with a smile. "He keeps trying to be right, or find out what is right in your eyes, so, when you can tell him, he can drop it and get on with other things."

"But I thought he just wanted someone to argue with him."

"He has that in his office. He doesn't want it at home."

"But he's always argued. Even in his parents' home they argued."

"Of course. That's how he was trained. He doesn't know any better. But inside him, he wants something else."

She stopped to think a minute, then continued. "But what do I do if he's wrong? You mean, I should agree with him?"

"Of course not. But don't push his nose in it. Continue the dialog. A discussion doesn't have to be an argument. Acknowledge that whatever he said may be one way of looking at something, and then help him think through to other ways."

"You mean lead him to the right one, like I do with my little boy."

I suppress a laugh at the look of disgust on her face. "No, I don't mean that. And you shouldn't be giving your son the 'you're wrong again' messages either. You can't really lead any man at any age. They're doers. They refuse to be led, even though some may fool you into believing they're listening to you and doing what you tell them to. However, you can inspire them, suggest things and elevate them. It lets them know you trust them to continue onward and upward."

"What if the path leads him off a cliff?"

"You'll find a way to turn him before that. That's the benefit of your insight, your second sight."

In the weeks that follow the retreat, she notices a big change in her husband and tells me he is much happier. I don't wonder why.

And I watch her become happier. She is standing beside him, not in front of him. And she notices he is beginning to stand beside her.

Not everyone reaches this understanding. Arguments can lead to confrontation and war.

She is sitting in front of me showing me bruises on her arms and shoulders. Her husband sits glumly across the room from her.

"He grabbed my arm and pushed me, then pulled me. It was awful." Her face is wet with tears.

"What started it?" I ask.

"We were talking about money. It always starts with money. I told him I was afraid we couldn't make the rent and then he started shouting at me and got real close to me. I put my arms up because I thought he was going to hit me. He grabbed my arm and that's all I remember."

"I just wanted her to be quiet. She was shouting, acting frantic and swinging at me," her husband inserts defensively.

She starts to cry again as he speaks. They have been lovers for several years and were recently married. He has hit her before and this has only recently come to light in our counseling sessions. Other lovers in her past have also physically abused her. I watch the panic in her eyes, her body slumping into hopelessness.

"I wanted this to be different..." she speaks weakly, her voice trailing off into thoughts of the past.

"It can be different, honey," he says, reaching across to take her hand in his. "I promise you it can be different. I love you. I will always love you."

I know she needs to be strong and establish boundaries so this won't happen again. But I know also that she has to realize her part in this, the things she unwittingly did to set this off, so the rage won't burst forth in him again.

"Do you love yourself?" I ask him.

He turns with a look of surprise. "Love myself? Well, I guess not. I mean, I always seem to fail her. I can't handle money very well at all. She's right."

"That's why I took over paying the bills," she inserts with liveliness in her voice. *"At least I get things covered with what little money we do have. If only he'd get a second job!"*

I ask her to hold her comments for a few moments while I complete something with him, and I turn my attention to him again. "What do you like about yourself?"

He thinks for quite some time. "Well, I'm good with kids, and I'm good on my job. And I have learned how to cool down when she gets me angry. I go outside and sit in my car or take a drive."

"So how come that didn't work this time?"

"She followed me out to my car and kept talking to me."

"Why didn't you just drive away?"

"I didn't want to leave her all upset like that, crying and shouting. I got out and tried to put my arms around her to hold her. And that's when it happened."

"You grabbed me and hurt me!" she shouts through tears.

"You were punching out at me. I tried to hold you and stop you," he counters. *"I guess I hurt you but I didn't mean to, honey."*

She turns away, speaking tearfully. "Well, you did hurt me. I have the bruises to prove it."

Now I must address her. "Do you remember what happened when you were talking to him and he got out of the car?"

"Yes. I was still talking about the money."

"And were you talking loudly?"

"Yes. I was excited... well, I was angry. He'd failed us again."

"And what did you think would happen? Did you realize he was getting angry too?"

"Yes. But I didn't expect him to hit me."

"I know. Then what happened when he reached out for you?"

"He was going to hit me!"

"But he held you instead, yes?"

"He was trying to restrain me."

"What was he saying, what were his words?"

"I don't know. He was saying something..."

He reached over and took her hand again. *"I was saying 'Honey, please stop. Please don't say those things to me.' I was trying to stop you because it hurt so much."*

I intervened and had them take time out. Later I started a major process of rebuilding their awareness of each other's love and marriage commitments.

Would it work? It would take time. Because it was not love that had been broken. It was trust. And trust once broken can never be given again in quite the same way. The age of innocence had passed.

The question here is not who was right and who was wrong. Both were right in some ways and wrong in others. Both had each other's buttons pushed down hard and would not let up.

For his part, he had tried to retreat from the fight. She had not let him go and he could not fully disengage either. He had to take responsibility for his anger, which he showed he was willing to do, and make positive efforts to change.

For her part, she had tried to take away the problem from him by taking over financial responsibility. Yet she had continued to rub his nose in his inadequacies, which destroyed his confidence further. This left him with the experience that his home was an unsafe place for him and he had to flee to his car.

And then she had done the one thing never to do – stand in front of the stampeding herd. It ran right over her.

The more the negativity builds between people, the less there is room for the positive. At some point, the relationship will break.

But consider this: what would have happened if the wife had simply stopped criticizing him and citing his inabilities?

Instead, she aired her own internal process and there was nothing that anyone outside her could do to stop her fears that she would not be supported. Her survival fears were far older than their relationship.

To him, her continual worries translated into a lack of trust in him. Perhaps his poor handling of affairs demonstrated that he was not worthy of her confidence. But that does not mean he was worthy of her distrust.

There was a very small window of hope in this relationship and I pursued it with them. The physical pushing and grabbing had to stop, but the anger had to stop first. She had to learn to stop standing in front of him and taunting him with her distrust. He had to learn to get on with his life, build his job and self-value, and stop trying to address all her worries.

They are still together a year later and still working on building trust. I have hope for them and they have hope for each other.

But please let me add a note of warning.

In any relationship, if angry behavior continues on the part of the man, and you cannot turn it away, then you must seek professional help. If that does not turn matters around, you must leave. Don't live in hope if you cannot change reality.

It is most important that the woman's grace and excellence be maintained. If the man challenges either one, and it cannot be quickly stopped, she incurrs is no karma by leaving the relationship. It is a matter of survival. For the sake of humanity, the woman must survive.

Many times women live in hope and disregard reality. When I see this happening with someone in an abusive situation, whether physical or psychological – and both are damaging – I help them establish thresholds. I walk her through the awareness of the painful abuse several times until she sees herself clearly and can accept that this is a reality she can no longer tolerate. While it is not a happy thing to do, it is necessary. Why? Because she has lost herself, she has no sense of self left to protect.

Only when a woman learns to live each day in her grace and excellence, only then does she stand a chance of being happy in this world.

Then the man stands a chance as well.

6

THERE ARE NO VICTIMS

I now know there are no victims.
We have created them in ourselves.

No one is to blame.
But we are all responsible.

There Are No Victims

The history of women for at least the last 3,000 years seems to be riddled with victims. One recalls the Biblical tale of the mob casting stones at the harlot and Jesus admonishing them to stop, with the words, "Let him who is without sin cast the first stone."

But no one ever cast stones at her aggressor – the man who first "defiled" her.

No one, at least, until this century.

Until the 1960s, when women turned out en masse to decry their slavery by men by burning their bras and demanding equal pay for equal time and a payscale for the housewife-mother whose duties had long gone unrewarded monetarily.

Within a decade, it was turnabout and men cried "Victim!" as the assault by women continued.

I was not among those bra-burning women, though I watched them with empathy from a distant window, ensconced in my first job in corporate America. I too felt the huge pay inequality and the sexual referencing that made me more valuable to my boss as "the best pair of legs in our department" than as the best set of brains.

But something seemed very wrong to me in all the protest. There was too much rage and too much blaming. Men hadn't made us this way, at least not all by themselves, I reasoned. Our mothers had a big hand in shaping who we are, just as their mothers did them.

Maybe we are all victims, I concluded. Maybe it's a chicken-and-egg thing and we'll never figure out who really deserves the blame. Or maybe we just blame God, blow it off, and go on about our business growing up.

Well, that was kind of what I did at that time, since there seemed time enough to put such unresolvable things on a back burner for later examination.

NO ONE IS TO BLAME

Now, more than thirty years later, I'm a counselor and teacher of women and life has taught me quite a bit more. Many of the women I work with would be classifiable as victims using those classic psychology textbooks. They marry victimizers, have children, become victimizers themselves, and continue the victim cycle.

But now, I know some things better than in the 1960s. For one thing, I now know there are no victims. We have created them in ourselves.

No one is to blame. But we are all responsible.

We just have to drop all that fine training we received that taught us how to be irresponsible. Other people do not exist for us to dump our responsibilities on.

Ask yourself this: Who got you up in the morning today? Your husband, your kid, or you? Sure, all of them, and maybe even the fear of losing a job and a paycheck. That all had a hand in your getting up. But don't use motivations and outside stimuli to obliterate the fact that it was you who chose to get up.

At every moment you have choice. And with each choice you make, you take responsibility for your life. If you prefer to think that you don't have choice, even *that* is your choice and you must take responsibility for that.

You may live your whole life choosing to say other people have made your life choiceless, but you can't get away with that forever. In the end, God and the Akashic Records - the permanent record of your deeds in all lifetimes - will remind you of that fact after this life is done. Believe me.

"Maybe it started when I was two, when my Mother beat me because I was crying and she was afraid I'd wake up Daddy and he'd beat her."

The face looking at me with eyes widened by the shock of many early-life traumas has just described what she believes was the onset of the victim cycle in her life. From that time on, she would have occurrences when she would no longer be responsible for her actions around men.

The smooth-lined male face sitting next to her is nearly in tears, agitated, and more than a bit angry at himself. He has hit her several times over the last few weeks and he cannot stand to think of himself as her abuser. "Like I'm some animal," he described himself. He loves her and he has just said so for the third time in this counseling session.

She listened to him but could not hear him, the voices were so loud in her head.

I watch her energy field, flat and sickly yellow with this old disease in her, lungs barely moving with each rapid breath drawn shallowly in and out of her throat.

"I have to take a bathroom break," I insert quickly into the conversation and add, looking at her, "Would you like to join me?"

She follows, un-thought-out words spilling from her lips as we enter the bathroom.

I turn and face her. "Look, you shouldn't be talking now. Your nervous system is fried. Your brain won't make sense, it's only babbling. The first thing you have to do is drink a lot of water, take a good long soak, take two or three baths or showers tomorrow, and start some long deep breathing. You have to rebuild."

"But I'm afraid of him. He'll just keep hitting me..." Her voice is somewhere between a sob and a scream.

"Yes, yes, I know what is happening. You need to put a little distance between you, just for a few days. Do you have a place you can stay for, say, a week?"

"Well, maybe I can call a friend."

"No, not a friend."

"Why not?"

"You'll only talk about the problem and keep it alive. You need a place to rebuild, not regroup for the next round of fighting. You need a place to build your nervous system, your basic physical and mental fiber, not somewhere where you can continue to be small."

I thought of our yoga center – the guest room there, and the daily yoga and meditations in the early morning hours she would enjoy - and I mentioned it as a possibility.

She said she would think about it and let me know in the morning. "Think about it" – that's a woman's alternative to saying "no" right off. Well, I smiled inwardly, if she has to think about it that long, she'll choose the friend.

*The next morning she calls me, having selected a friend
to stay with. I give her an assignment involving
breathing exercises and some yoga postures to rebuild
the nervous system and aura, and a few mind-focusing
tasks. If she does any of them she'll be the stronger for
it and we can continue to rebuild herself and her
marriage.*

My first orientation is to rebuild the woman, not the
marriage. If I can help make the woman strong, living in her
own excellence, her marriage and everything in her
environment will be the better for it. Many counselors strive
to patch a relationship together with communications
techniques and other highly valuable skills, but without
direct work first on the woman, the patchwork-quilt sooner
or later frays apart again.

It is the woman whose fibers must be rebuilt if anything
else in her life is to make sense and endure.

And what do you do with the man in this process? You
prop him up with some type of mental baling wire, work
swiftly and pray he'll hold together long enough for her to
come around. Each relationship has its own window which,
when it closes, can rarely ever be opened again for the
couple to come back together.

HOW DOES THIS HAPPEN?

Nearly all women believe they are wounded, less than
whole, or lacking something. Many keep themselves going
despite it, using strong daily practices of a physical and
emotional nature, even devoting their energies to some good
cause, and only occasionally reflecting on this inner fault.

But in many cases, women dwell on this inner wounding too long. This leaves them wide open for physical and emotional abuse. How does this happen?

Now we're talking strictly yogic energy science, tapping into precious gems given us by Yogi Bhajan.

The self-esteem of a person is reflected in the strength of a part of the auric field called the "arc line," which sits like a cap or helmet directly over the top of the head extending up and outward a few inches. Traditionally drawn auras around the heads of Christian saints in sacred artwork actually depict the arc line as the halo.

A man has only one arc line, over the head – since he is a creature of the head or ego and requires power there. A woman has two of these, one over the head and the other arcing like a rainbow over her heart. She is a creature of the heart and needs the additional power there.

The balance of the aura above the arc line and around the whole body – extending out nine to fifteen feet – gives protection to both sexes, providing of course that the aura is dense and strong and charged with positive energy.

Now what determines the strength of both the arc line and the aura? The strength of the body inside – not just the organs and physical systems but also the mind and the emotions.

Ugly, dark thoughts punch black holes in the aura. Promises made and not kept blow the heck out of the energy field. A life spent in complaints shrivels up auric strength.

All this lets other energies in. What energies? Everything we're living around – people's dark thoughts, cluttered minds, envy, rage, and so forth. If a person has no regular spiritual practice to rebuild and cleanse the energy fields, that gunk just keeps piling up.

Now consider the differing elemental natures of both sexes that we discussed earlier.

Which of the two sexes involves itself more in deep processes, stewing and chewing over thoughts endlessly? Right – the woman. Which sex is more likely to be fired up into action, moving and breathing hard and pulling in all that universal energy stuff we call prana and therefore building the strength of the aura? Right again – the man.

So who is more likely to feel themselves the victim of others' abuse? The woman. Simply because the woman is more open.

A LIFELONG PROBLEM OF LETTING GO

In addition, the woman has a lifelong problem letting go. Yogi Bhajan has often described how the woman has an imprintable aura and men do not. This holds particular significance in relationships.

What this means is simple: in intimate exchanges, most especially sexual in nature, the woman's aura picks up and holds the imprint of the man like film in a camera. This process begins to happen with the first sexual encounter. So much for casual sex!

It is a woman's greatest challenge not to engage intimately without gaining a true commitment.

How long does it take to "divorce" a man's energy from your aura, if you're a woman? It can take up to nine years, particularly if you continue to think of the person or see him again and again. Properly instructed, however, a woman can cleanse her aura using meditation in about a year.

For almost all women this truth prevails: *every man you have slept with over the past nine years is still with you.*

Now what about the man's aura? Quite the opposite of a woman. In intimate relationships, the man is like a camera without film. His aura retains little of her presence.

This is the simple energy-field understanding why men find it far easier than women to have multiple sexual partners. Her aura would be cluttered with imprints, confusing her on the subconscious level if not the conscious. His aura is built for action and so off he goes!

How could nature be so seemingly cruel to a woman, you might ask? Well, for one thing, women are designed by Nature to hold on to some important things – for instance, babies, knowledge and sensitivities so she can be warned and wary of oncoming challenges.

Do you know that, after a mother becomes attuned to her baby's presence, she can sense that her child is in trouble 250 miles away?

If a woman chooses to make a commitment to a man, she has to help him develop a higher level of commitment to her than mere sexual bonding. Men without a steady spiritual practice are rarely able to make and hold on to such a commitment.

Without such a commitment, his bond to her will last no more than two-four weeks. She would have to maintain a constant emotional presence in his energy field until he becomes visually and kinesthetically centered on her.

Now some folks might bring up the fact that a man can stay fixated on a woman he chases for a very long time, which might seem to conflict with a lack of imprintable aura. To the contrary, it supports it. It is the man's goal-driven ego, which has been captured. The fall-off effect comes after the conquest if she fails to convince him that she can meet more than his sexual needs.

So now imagine Woman as a young girl and see how abuse can begin early. Imagine a two or three-year-old, her mother weak and complaining with a consequently weak aura unable to protect her from a father's advances. The mother is most likely unaware of those advances.

"I can remember when my Father cornered me in my bedroom right before I was to marry my first husband," the middle-aged woman is telling me.

I have seen her for a half-dozen sessions and she is still trying to recoil from what another therapist told her was sexual abuse by her father when she was a three-year-old child. She never believed the therapist. Her only sexual encounter with her father occurred at nineteen, which she is describing to me now.

"What did he actually do to you?" I ask.

"He pushed me down on the bed and tried to pull my skirt off. He didn't get very far because my Mother walked in."

"What did she do?"

"Nothing. He got up real quickly and started talking about something or other. She was talking too, and I think they were both pretending that nothing had happened."

"Did you say anything to her?"

"No. Nothing had really happened. At least that's what I tried to believe then."

"But your father had assaulted you."

"Yes, yes..." she started to sob. "I wish I could remember if he had touched me when I was little..."

"What would it do for you if you could remember something?"

The question startled her and she looked at me not quite comprehending what I had asked. I repeated the question.

Through her tears the answer came. "Then I would know... I would know...if I should really hate him."

That's what knowing would do for some of us – make it okay to hate. And what would hate do for us?

THE CYCLE OF HATE

Continuing the cycle of hate – that is what continuing the victim cycle is doing to us, producing multi-generational hatred passed on from parents to children. The abused mother helps to create an abused daughter, who then becomes a mother herself and fans the flames of hatred in her husband, who vents it by abusing their child.

Often the mother pretends not to notice, not to acknowledge that the same thing is happening to her daughter. At times she may blame the child, beat her, accuse her of seduction. In all cases, the child grows up to continue the cycle herself.

The fault, dear friends, lies not in our genes, but in our mental programs.

The social help structure is set up to continue this exploration into self-hatred and other-hatred. Therapists deftly explore clients' histories seeking out the bad news – rarely the good news. They concentrate on women whose psyches and energy fields are so impressionable.

What good does it do to confront people with garbage? It can take years to clean it up. Where, with all this confrontation and provocation, is the uplift? Where is the inspiration?

Where do we learn the Truth – the Truth, not the facts? *The Truth is that we are not garbage. We are not products of garbage. We are the flowers, the princesses, the grace of humanity.*

Certainly, we do not hear this Truth about who women really are in most churches and temples. Not where they preach sin.

Not in families, where you are reminded of the continuing mess you're in.

Not even in many self-help groups, such as incest-survivor groups or other recovery programs. For all the obvious good such groups do, unfortunately they continue to support the woman's belief that she is "broken" and a "victim" with the continual regurgitation of their garbage history.

But continually convincing us we're sinners, we're garbage, we're inferior, broken goods is what keeps us under control. Yes, virtually everything in society is set up to keep women under control.

Don't ask why. The answers will only make you angrier, more enraged. In reality, the only real answer to the why question can come from God in meditation and prayer.

The soul's lessons are many and take courage to endure. Our pain and problems were supposed to turn us inward to discover our strengths, not to rip up our guts, make us rage at others and deaden our senses.

Asking how things got this way – this mass control of women – is quite a different question than why, and gives us clues on how to get out of it and go beyond.

It was generous of me in the 1960s to conclude that we are all victims. That way I could accept that all humanity, men and women, are trapped in the same game.

In reality, we are in the same game – all learning to throw off the label of victim.

VICTIMS ARE MADE, NOT BORN

Victims are made, not born. They can be un-made. No one has to be a victim unless they continue to make themselves so. The victim role stops the moment you make a choice you really want to choose. Any choice, about anything you want to choose. Just start!

Yes, cruel things happen to children growing up. But once you achieve some stage of adulthood, adopting a model of self-responsibility can help build the real you, the "You" you really are and want to be. That doesn't mean putting on a fake face for others, but rather a real face to present to ourselves every day – a brighter, kinder one.

Each of us must become something other than the sum of our childhood programs. We must drop the naïveté that got us into victim situations.

"I was only eleven years old, but I was precocious for my age. That's why my parents let me take the subway alone downtown to my music lesson each week."

The face looking at me could have been my own – a woman in her 50s, only now becoming aware of the sexual problems she faced as a child growing up in the late 1940s.

"It was great fun, being on my own. After my lesson, I would stop off at the main library, browsing in the stacks, pretending I was a little foreign traveler visiting

there for the first time. I would approach the librarian. Admittedly, I was always a little scared she would accuse me of being a pretender. I would ask her for a certain book in my best fake French accent and with the best etiquette that my Philadelphia upbringing could muster. It was scary and enormous fun.

"Then I would head toward the subway, past penny arcades and some rather trashy stores, and stop at a certain newsstand that sold comic books. Occasionally, I'd buy one, even though I was forbidden to read them, and later I'd sneak it into the house inside one of my school books."

I could tell the tense part was coming by the lines accumulating on her forehead as she was speaking.

"Then, one afternoon, coming from the library after a particularly exciting foray into my role playing, somehow I couldn't drop the little French girl character. The thrill of it took me over. I was no longer walking down this dirty street by these arcades; I was this little French girl here for a visit and my curiosity was leading me into strange new places.

"Timidly, I stepped inside the arcade. It was narrow and deep and the walls were lined with pinball machines with a few men playing them. I walked over to one where there was no one and examined it as if seeing such a machine for the first time. My finger traced an imaginary route the ball would go if I hit it.

"Suddenly a man's voice spoke up close behind me. He was asking me if I wanted a quarter to play the game. I gathered my wits and replied 'No, thank you,' with my best French accent. He asked me where I was from. I

told him Paris – I didn't really know any other city in France – and I added that I was just visiting for a short time with my Aunt. That sounded more sophisticated than saying parents.

"He said he'd show me how to play the game and, before I realized what was happening, he had moved behind me, his arms circling around me, taking my right hand in his to pull back on the device that released the first pinball. For a few seconds I felt a giddy rush up my spine to the back of my head, and then I felt his body pressing up against mine and heard his breath heavy in my ear. The smell of alcohol on him was so heavy it stifled my own breath.

"I tried to push away from him but his body molded around me in first one direction then another. He laughed at the sport of it. I wanted to cry out but the scream was locked inside me. Panic set in as I vainly tried to continue playing the game. He pressed against me harder. Suddenly he started coughing and as his body convulsed backward I pushed away from him, running out the arcade, hearing his voice behind me calling me as he pursued.

"I ran with all my strength down the crowded sidewalk, pushing roughly past people, my hat flying off my head, not even daring to look back.

"Ahead of me was the familiar newsstand, and the face of my friend who sold me a comic every week. Startled, he looked down at me as I rushed up to him.

"'Quick, you've got to help me,' I shouted at him. 'There's a man chasing me. Please, please stop him.'

"And I rushed on. Running all the way down the steps to the subway. Not even looking back as the subway doors closed behind me and I sat down in a back seat behind dozens of anonymous faces.

"I could still hear his laughter, even though I knew it was no longer near me. I would hear his laughter the rest of my life.

"What a fool I had been. What a silly, naïve, stupid fool."

Yes, she was naïve. And as such, unaware and unconscious of the hunter-prey games played in sexual combat. Living life unconsciously is what makes most women victims in such games.

She had avoided actual physical harm. Some would say there was little to scar. But she was scared. She was the victim of psychic rape.

She had not been trained. She was raised by well-meaning, but equally untrained parents who did not tell her not to take the hand of a stranger. She was raised by the movies of post-war America where the coquettish young woman had all the fun and excitement, and the consequences were never filmed. Only lived and never talked about.

Thus we were trained, and then shocked, saddened and sickened by the consequences of such games played in the real world. We grew up angry, robbed early of our childhood and feeling somehow defiled. More and more young women actually were.

The celluloid myths of our innocent puberty were depicted in the film "Seven Brides for Seven Brothers," a mass abduction shown without defilement that was seen as sweet and ended in seven "marriages." Those innocent nuggets came and went, and another all-too-real world began to appear, beginning with "Splendor in the Grass" where the consequences of our naïveté were filmed and shown.

Who were these men, these brutes? Surely they weren't the same men as our brothers, our fathers. Didn't they know we were only playing?

Women became even harder, turning to punishing men with their anger, tempting them on, then pulling away, and raising rage in men which they had never known or seen before. The world became the reality of "Saturday Night Fever," lived for passion and defilement and ending in suicide.

Why are women so overwhelmingly the ones who are physically hurt in this cruel game, generally not men?

Because women are no match for men in rage. Women in rage are the seducers and slow torturers who can hold onto rage for years. Men in rage are the killers who can strike in an instant. Rage is the shadow side of the man.

Both men and women have learned how to live as victims and both suffer.

It is unfortunate that generations of women – perhaps from time immemorial – have been reared to believe that they are somehow incomplete without a man. While it is helpful to focus on partnering for the growth that can come through sharing, no statement regarding a woman could be further from the truth.

It has led women to become used by men, to be labeled as "babes" and "bimbos" and "dames" and not as their unique, whole and beautiful selves. And every time a woman accepts being called such a nameless-name, she moves one step further into the victim circle.

She becomes universalized as needy, incomplete, weak and secondary. She becomes an object, a thing, soon to be used up and lifeless.

Bimbos and babes, chicks and dames,
They are the women nobody names,
Nobody looks to for love or advice,
No one remembers for virtue or vice.

Women of vanity, women of fear,
succumbing to insanity when men are near,
painted and pampered, yet angry their face,
far from their excellence, far from their grace.

One day they'll wake when gray is their hair,
barely remembering, but dimly aware
that once they were children who hadn't a care,
once they believed they were going somewhere.

They must revive now to start a new day,
recapture the heart they gave away,
throw out the rage, brush off the tear,
smile through their anger and bury their fear.

Then will the angels dance with delight,
that women have awakened to their might,
leading themselves and others to come
out of the dark and into the sun.

"Victims No More!"
Sangeet Kaur Khalsa

7

THE TRUTH ABOUT THE GOOD OLD GIRL NETWORK

The only secret to being liked
is to like yourself first,
whether or not anyone else does.

Then you're safe from others' control
because you're safe from
your own neediness.

The Truth About
The Good Old Girl Network

There comes a time when we all need to cry, a time when we need to talk out our problems. That's the single most important reason why most women have women friends.

You have worries and somebody has to listen.

Unfortunately, when you do this you'll find that you simply build the problem. The more you talk about your problem the bigger it gets.

But if you have to discuss it, don't tell it to a man, at least not often or for very long. A man will try to "fix" you, and women by their nature are so complex they defy fixing. So eventually he will resent your complaints, and look on you as weak and ignorant.

Instead, talk to a woman, but choose a mature woman – one who can help you find solutions and new options and behaviors, not one who will envy or ridicule you or lay her own private agenda on you.

Finding such a woman isn't easy.

"I found myself instantly feeling for her, listening to her story and realizing she grew up with the same problems I did, and now she was going through the same mess in her marriage that I was."

The young woman speaking to me has just told me she is divorcing her husband of three years. She is hardly

30, and her husband only a year older. They are both on their second divorce.

"So then what happened?" I asked.

"Theresa and I both decided to file for our divorces the same day," she answered.

"For the same reasons?"

"Basically, yes. Neither of our husbands really cared for us – they took us for granted. We were just carpets emotionally for them."

I saw the key when her answers switched to "we" and there was no separation between them. Rarely are any two situations truly identical. This seemed like a think-alike case to me.

"Didn't you have a birthday a couple of weeks ago?" I asked.

"Yes, but what's that got to do with anything?"

"Oh, I just wondered what Tad did to celebrate your birthday."

"We just went out to dinner, that's all," she answered a little defensively.

"And nothing else? Didn't he give you a present?"

"Some flowers, and..." her words came to a grinding halt.

"And something else?"

"Well, he did give me a pair of plane tickets, for us to go to Hawaii for a special vacation."

"That sounds nice. And is that something he does regularly?"

"No. We haven't been on a vacation like that since we went on our honeymoon..." Her eyes started to glaze over with tears.

"Maybe he wanted to please you. Maybe he knew you were feeling down about you and him..."

"But Theresa said..."

"Theresa probably said something like, 'My husband did that too and tried to buy me off with some pretty present but that didn't work – I saw through him...' Was it something like that?"

"Yes...but she only meant to console me."

"I'm sure she did. Was that when you decided to file for a divorce?"

"Yes."

"Would you like to rethink your decision now?"

Over the next couple of sessions, we discussed the facts leading up to her judgement of her marriage. We gradually separated her case from that of her friend. The marriage began to heal and they had a second chance.

Interestingly enough, she shared her new learning with Theresa who, at first, was hurt to think her friend believed her to be the "bad guy." Later, she conceded she had learned a few things and perhaps she should reconsider her divorce decision as well.

Think-alike still continued, but at least on a happier note.

Most women seek others' opinions because they don't know their own. They don't know how to find it, or how to talk to themselves, and it doesn't often occur to them to talk to God. They think that by talking to others they will figure out their own answers.

The problem is: at times they just take on others' answers as their own. Their answers and their problems. And so the problems can compound themselves.

Women basically don't like to think alone, or go somewhere alone – just as one woman leaving a table to go to the bathroom will invite other women to join her and one or two will automatically rise to do that, with no second thought.

That is not because they want to talk – though the bathroom trip is often an opportunity to chat.

Women simply possess group consciousness, while men more often exemplify the "lone-hunter" consciousness.

In fact, "wanting to talk" has often been a woman's excuse for getting together.

It never ceases to amaze men how much women love to talk. Few women understand how men are rarely prepared to match them in communications.

Men's frustration comes because women are almost always in the middle of their own mental processes and that is obvious when they talk. Few men have the time or patience to wade through the processing with them.

Men laugh about the way women get together to talk, and they try to make a joke of it. In India, women in some communities have a tradition of getting together every afternoon to talk. They call it the daily "peanut hour", because they like to gobble up spicy nuts and snacks during their daily gatherings.

THE CONTINUAL COMPARISON GAME

What makes life so difficult for women relating to other women is their comparing mind. She cannot stop comparing herself, her parts, and her environment to that of other women and almost always seeing herself the loser in the comparison.

The first time I heard Yogi Bhajan point this out at a women's camp, a whole lot of things began to make sense to me about women.

For instance, I could see how this comparison thing gives rise to envy – a state of feeling few men know anything about.

The comparison game goes on continually. Watch a group of women naked together in a shower, or in bathing suits on a beach. "She's got better legs than me," one thinks to herself, feeling less than beautiful and perfect.

You see, women are continually comparing themselves to other women. They can't help it, it's that automatic. "She's got a better husband," or "I make more money than her," or "She's got a better car than me."

It's the "more-better-thinner-richer-less-worse-fatter-poorer game" and it's a woman's downfall. Because it leaves each woman always feeling unsure of herself – kind of like "the fastest gun in the West" who is proud of his title but always lives in fear of when the next sharpshooter will come around the corner who may be faster.

It is a strange paradox that women will seek out each other's advice and counsel even though they often don't like each other, even in fact when they feel envy for each other, and compare themselves to each other to their own detriment.

Who sets the standards of comparison? Ironically, women themselves. Oh yes, they do buy into what the man-in-their-life may tell them about themselves, and they continually look for compliments from him to bolster up their insecure self-images. But, in reality, each woman is the supreme, and often harshest, judge of herself.

If she has a low opinion of herself, she may do anything to keep herself down – such as surround herself with obviously pretty girlfriends so she can think herself as unattractive. Or she may do anything to try to bolster her self-opinion – such as sabotage a friend's marriage, diet, choice of dress or hairstyle.

If she has a high opinion of herself, she is equally dangerous to others and supports her self-image in a similar manner. She may choose homely companions and do all she can to keep them homely, or she may poach in a girl friend's marital territory.

The basic truth is: if a woman feels she has little or nothing, she will either make her condition worse or try to improve it – all by external means. In past decades, it was a common joke that when a woman felt depressed she just went out and bought a new hat. Now, she may go out and get a new husband – especially at another woman's expense.

How could a woman with high self-esteem be capable of doing the same things? Because she is never ever sure of herself. She is always open to the pitfalls of the comparison game.

It is far worse than looking at yourself in a mirror. When you accept the opinions of others about you, it is akin to accepting yourself as the mirror image. Others can never know who you are on the inside, so they judge you by mostly superficial, circumstantial evidence.

Many women, however, are stuck on the inside – inside, with their own negative beliefs about themselves. No amount of compliments, no amount of "new hats" can pull them out. To make that even more complicated, most women have some belief that somewhere deep down inside there's something wrong or missing or just not right. So how can they win?

Buy as many hats as they can, get as many husbands as they can, they can never believe in themselves. Because nothing from the outside works.

And the more they talk about their problems, the worse things look on the inside.

A MATTER OF TRUST

The problem is few, if any, women really trust themselves.

What is trust? It is a constant experience of dependability – a history of experiences that tell you, 'You can depend on yourself!' Most women experience only that they cannot depend on themselves. They have been trained to fail themselves on their own, and therefore to need others.

"You are great but you do not have a great capacity to experience your greatness."

When I first heard Yogi Bhajan say that to a group of women I sat bolt upright at attention. He was talking about us! Women – we were great.

Over the years I have come to understand just how important it is to incorporate this belief in our self perception.

This greatness is a woman's basic character. But how does she use it – to bring herself up or down? Frequently her great capacity is used to experience and remind herself of her weakness, her wrongness, and her not-good-enoughness.

So women look to other women as friends they can "trust." What do they trust them for? They trust other women to be like themselves – perhaps a little better in one or two things (there's that old comparison game again!) – but still like themselves, basically flawed.

That is why women rely on women as friends – it is "safe." They can understand and listen to each other because they are linked by common flaws. And that is why women trust men more, because they think men are not flawed like them. Therefore they believe men must be the ones who have this capacity for greatness, at least in greater measure than it appears to be in women.

And so women make a basic mistake and revise their behavior patterns in an attempt to gain strength from men. Either they model themselves after men and compete with them in business, or they cash in on their so-called womanly prowess and seduce a powerful man to shelter them.

This drive has drawn a good part of a generation of women into the workplace, taking up men's competitive games and men's values, many becoming near-men. As a result, they are rewriting women's medical history, having stress attacks and heart attacks and other historically male anger-based problems.

The balance of women have become second-class citizens living under the protectorate of men, in marriages which will most likely not last more than a few years.

Either way, the woman-fiber of Western culture is being greatly diminished. Those who go into business dance with the potential of becoming male-like in the competitive fray. Those who do not, become weakened by self-distrust and try to win by living in servitude to men.

A FRIEND IN NEED INDEED!

So the question arises, can a woman truly be a friend if she has fallen into either trap? The answer is no – not to other women and certainly not to men. Because she is not a friend to herself. She is a judge and critic of herself, and as such, unpredictable and untrustworthy. She is envy personified.

Think of that marvelous story "Cinderella." You can tear it apart for all its woman-needs-man, man-rescues-woman scenarios, but this cute little story is a blueprint for envy. Women - the hateful stepsisters - envying and hating poor little Cinderella.

When Cinderella is "discovered" by her prince, what do you think suddenly turns her sisters into adoring fans? Have they seen the light of higher consciousness? Hardly! They simply want to be on the winning side, in case someone throws a few bones their way.

All too often, the game of love is the game of have and have not, where those women who "have" zealously guard their territory against the poaching actions of those "have not" women around them. Often such poachers come dressed in the guise of a friend.

For such a woman, this is often not a conscious act on her part. She may even shock herself when she finds herself sexually involved with her "best friend's" husband.

The theme of betrayal among women is historic - far older than the lament in the song "Missouri Waltz" - and in some social strata it is on the increase.

"I thought all those despicable women I see on TV talk shows were fake, or at least not anyone I would ever know," Marsha told me with anger the first time she came to my office. "And then I found out my husband had been cheating on me with another woman for years, from virtually the month after we married."

When she brought her husband in to see me, to tell his side of the story, he was in tears. All he could say was,

" I don't know how it happened. And then I couldn't get out of it."

Marsha wanted to blame the "other woman." He wanted to blame himself, and Marsha also feared she herself was to blame. In reality, they were all responsible.

Marsha had rested on her laurels and didn't see the telltale signals. Her husband liked being admired and courted and left himself open prey to an office romance. And the "other woman" told herself the classic lie that he would leave Marsha and marry her.

Eventually he did pull away from the other woman. She sent an accusatory letter – with photos – to Marsha, designed to blow the marriage apart.

It was at that point that they came to see me.

"What do I do?" he asked me.

"Tell Marsha the truth."

"I have."

"I mean the whole truth." I looked at him squarely in the eyes. "Tell Marsha what that letter doesn't say."

Slowly and painfully I got him to tell me the whole story, piece by piece. And then I made him promise to tell Marsha. "It is only practical," I told him, "since this other woman could write it all to her anyway."

"But won't that give her more to worry about and feel bad about?" he offered.

"She's already imagining as much or more than you could tell her," I answered. "Tell her, 'This is the whole

truth, all of it, and then tell the story.' Then end with a long hug and hold her like you mean it."

"I do mean it. I love her."

"Fine. Let her feel it."

I reminded him of how he felt and what he did when he was courting Marsha, and he said he wanted to do all that and more to win her back. I knew he meant it. My only concern was, what would happen after he did?

When Marsha came to see me I had to first wake her up to understand that it was her husband's neediness that made him vulnerable. And there are always needy women around.

"So this could happen again?" she asked.

"Yes, it could," I said honestly. "I won't lie to you."

"Maybe we should just get a divorce now and end it." She slumped in the chair with a defeated look.

"Maybe you should just roll over and die – is that what you want? Remember the good times you've had together. You can have more again. You just have to be wiser."

"But I can never trust him again," she said with tears flowing down her cheeks.

"You can never take him for granted again," I countered. "Man is forever the hunter. You must always be a little elusive, never completely conquered, still a bit mysterious, playful and fun."

"And what about her? I know her. I've met her at office parties. What do I say to her?"

"Don't answer the letter. If she calls, refer the call to your husband. Let him handle her. Don't engage her and let yourself be vulnerable to your own emotions as well as hers."

"But I hate her!" she scowled darkly at me. "I loathe her."

I smiled at her look. "Then she has won and you have lost."

"What do you mean?"

"She got your goat. Do you know the expression, 'If I can't have him, nobody else can have him either'?" She nodded her head. "Well she's set out to destroy – you, him, the marriage, anything she can. Now look at the tactic. If she really had him in her pocket, would she try to hurt him? No. She's acting like the woman scorned and this is all her fury. So you've won. Don't throw it all away now."

"You mean he really prefers me?"

"Yes. You're the one he comes home too. He could have left a long time ago. He's been trying to extract himself from her web for quite some time. You've heard the truth from him, right?"

"Yes, I guess so."

"Yes, you know so. Did you not see the pain on his face? It came from his heart. He never wanted to hurt you. That was why he didn't break it off sooner, trying to keep her at bay so you would be safe."

Over the next month, the marriage was slowly patched back together. But I knew it was only a matter of time before the issue would come up again for him, because he had not addressed his own neediness.

Marsha had slipped back into the role of making him comfortable at home and taking him for granted. His thoughts slipped back to the excitement of seeing the other woman. He came to me fearing that he would soon act on his compulsion to call her.

"What will talking to her do for you?" I asked.

"I don't know. I guess I just want to know that she's all right, that she doesn't hate me."

"So you want her to forgive you?"

"I guess so."

"She won't, and you know that. You'll stir up her rage again and really muddy the waters. Do you want her to beat you up?"

"It hurts when I see her in the office sometimes and she avoids my eyes. I find myself staring at her back darting down a hallway."

"Don't bury yourself and your marriage with this guilt. Let it go. Let her go, now."

I started to work with him in a series of processes to help him define what he wanted in his life – at first to take his mind off her. More importantly, I wanted to help him tap into other areas in his life to get what had dragged him into this affair – excitement, adventure, respect and admiration.

Over time, he started to make changes in the way he did business, and the way he talked with people. He started to like himself more.

"The only secret to being liked is to like yourself first, whether or not anyone else does," I told them both at one point. "Then you do things a certain way because you like yourself. You live honestly with yourself and like your life. Then you're safe from others' control because you're safe from your own neediness."

The final piece was for Marsha to stop being haunted by the face of the other woman.

One day she called me up to tell me she had hidden the offending photos from sight, where no one would ever find them. I told her she still knew where they were, and so they weren't far enough away. She asked me if I would take them and I declined, saying that would be a cop-out. We both laughed over that one.

Then, on the anniversary of their marriage, her husband wrote her a song and played it on his guitar. She cried on his shoulder, he hugged her warmly, and she slept soundly with him that night. Several nights later, they burned the photos. Now when she occasionally sees her in the office, she offers a polite smile. The smile of a winner.

A SPECIAL CONNECTION BETWEEN "SISTERS"

There is a special link between women that can be quite the opposite – it can be supportive, happy, loving. A true sisterhood.

No woman has ever completely broken the link with the first woman in her life, Mother. Whether it was happy or traumatic or some combination of both, she feels a special connection with that love potential from many women she will know throughout her life.

As she matures she may meet some special sister who feels for her like no one ever has before.

The face of the young woman sitting across from me is flushed with excitement and confusion. She has just had a strange yet beautiful experience with a close friend whom she now recognizes as a true "sister."

They had been at a large party together and a man had tried to force her into an empty bedroom. He had been rough with her and she had only gotten away by being forceful, obstinate and verbally nasty.

Her friend had left the party with her and they had sat for hours. She had told her friend about an incident in her childhood when a relative had abused her and the fear and ugliness of it had never left her.

"I sat in that car and cried my eyes out, and I never do that. I never let myself be seen upset in any way."

I nodded my head for her to continue.

"Then she just held me, and as I was crying I heard someone else crying and I looked up at her face and saw it was her. She was crying with me and for me. No one has ever cried for me, not ever, not even my own Mother. For the first time I knew that someone understood me, felt my pain. It was a bit scary but it was beautiful."

Together they built a deep friendship. They found they could talk out their problems and neither one would judge the other. They could share each other's happy times and neither would feel envy or jealousy.

This is the way the best of relations between women can and does work. No judgement, no comparisons, no envy, just warmth and understanding. That is what women long for when they hang out with other women, whether or not they are consciously aware of it. That is what they try to get from men, and do not recognize that a woman is better suited to give them that depth of understanding. Men will try to fix or change them.

That is the potential underlying the good old girl network – a sisterhood of love without game-playing. Now, more and more women are discovering it.

That is how things are becoming, but it hasn't always been that way.

NATURAL ALLIES

Let me give you some historical perspective on the roles women have played with each other in the second half of this century. This comes from my own personal record.

I knew many women but had few women friends when I was growing up. The reason was simple: growing up in the '40s and '50s was a time when almost all young women were geared toward, and trained to, entrap men. Therefore, relations with other women were secondary if not altogether unimportant.

The soda fountain was a place where young people hung out – young men looking for and making eyes at young women bunched together at tables, giggling and waiting to be selected.

There was safety in numbers so they bunched together at public places and around school. Friendships with women made under those circumstances were tenuous – lasting until the "big romance" came around. Woman-to-woman relations usually fell into two categories: either they were allies in the entrapment game, or competitive threats. The exceptions, of course, were those of us who were dubbed "eggheads" – we just didn't exist as players in the game.

I still remember leaning out my college dorm window in 1956 to watch two women artfully breaking the lock on the trunk of a car so that they could get some gullible young man to fix it, claiming they could not.

What cleverness it took to appear to be so weak, I thought. Women had to be very good at lying about themselves. And what did they get for it? A man they had trapped. Who would want such a man? I wondered, as I turned back to my music and books.

The 1960s brought an awakening of consciousness on many levels – politically, environmentally, and sexually. The Beatles and other Rockers brought more than a new sound of freedom. They brought an independence not just to couples dancing but to the larger consciousness of coupling.

I for one could finally express myself on the dance floor without having to try to match a less-nimble-footed partner.

But something else was growing between women. Call it a sisterhood, a new form of "natural allies" that had little to do with the old entrapment game.

It was the beginning of our time to wake up, to lead a new consciousness, to have a voice that was heard socially and politically.

It was the start of women's rights, the birth of charismatic politicians like New York's Bella Abzug with her preposterous hats and fiery speeches. It was Sonny and Cher, Ike and Tina Turner, and a host of black women blues singers who didn't need a man around to be great.

Suddenly the music changed, seemingly overnight, from co-dependent songs like "You're Nobody 'til Somebody Loves You" and "All Alone by the Telephone" to "Proud Mary" and other loud blasting pieces that heralded the birth of a "new babe" who was nobody's baby anymore.

Not everybody hopped on the new bandwagon, of course. That would take a couple of decades before the tricksters, the babes and the sweeties would see the folly of their games and start living like whole people expecting whole people as mates.

The first wave of free women hit men like a kick in the groin. Men were what was wrong with the social condition! Some radical feminists even refused to associate with men on the job. It would be a decade or more before women, in their quiet time, going beyond their pain, would realize that men weren't the problem. After all, both men and women had been raised by Moms and Dads who themselves didn't know any better.

There were scads of secrets their mothers never told them, because their mothers never knew those secrets.

The public stage of change was taken up with large issues at first – the outcry against racism and the Vietnam War. Then the human rights of an even more vast class of individuals came forward with the women's movement.

Our pain at being disenfranchised, given second class jobs and no-class family roles became a marching banner and, at last, a uniting song. It would be a couple of decades until Helen Reddy would pen the song, "I Am Woman!", but the seeds were being sown.

They met in a folk bar on New York's Lower East Side almost every evening. They listened to singers strum guitars and sing out against the war. Phil Ochs was their favorite and they came whenever he played. They held hands when no one was watching. They fell in love. Their names were Estelle – Essie for short – and Adele.

Estelle was a survivor of Auschwitz, having been only a small child there while her parents struggled to live through the horrors, including the death-by-starvation of their young son in the camp. The youngest friends Estelle remembered were a pair of rats that visited her under her bunk at night. Eventually even they starved to death, even though she brought them morsels of bread whenever she could. She still cried when she talked about them.

I knew Essie in college, and I remained her friend when we both moved to New York. I often joined her to listen to and enjoy Phil Ochs.

Adele was born in Holland at about the same time as Essie. She remembered the time when her parents and the whole community put on the colored armbands of Jews in defiance of the Nazi roundup of Jewish Dutch citizens. She was petrified that she would be taken away. When she was not, she felt guilty that she had hidden while so many others were captured each time the Nazis swept through their street.

The war became a series of painful moments, as so many of her friends were taken away, never to be seen again. She could only imagine the horrors of the places they were sent to, told in the whispered stories heard by her parents and overheard by her.

One evening, Essie said simply to Adele, "I love you." They hugged and Adele responded with, "I love you." And so they moved in together in a small fourth floor walkup on a nameless street off Broadway on Manhattan's Upper West Side.

It was easy to live together in those days – women were discovering each other as friends, and some quietly as lovers, in cities all across the country.

They were happy together, even blissful. They attended an occasional meeting held by "the Movement" with dozens of other women, but they never went on marches. They preferred to keep quietly by themselves.

I also discovered my first close woman friend, Rose. We met on a job, became instantly close and went everywhere together. Though we were not intimates like Essie and Adele, we often joined them for a night out. Neither of us thought anything about the two of them holding hands or hugging. It all seemed natural.

Rose and I didn't join them at the gay clubs and they didn't join us at parties where there were men – not because of judgement but out of preference.

It would have been easy, I thought, to slip into a physical relationship with a woman like Rose. The nurturance was something I had never found in a man. But I just couldn't imagine myself ever marrying anyone other than a man. Neither could Rose. I liked the balance of energies, man to woman. So I took the nurturance of friendship and the hugs that women shared easily and publicly.

And then one day my relationship with Essie and Adele changed forever. It came with a simple announcement from Essie.

"We're going to have a baby," was all she said.

"A baby? Who – you?"

She laughed. "No, I wouldn't have the patience for nine months. Adele is pregnant."

"And who is the father?" I asked incredulously.

"What does it matter who the father is?" Her voice was tinged with anger.

"Well it may some day matter to the child."

"I doubt it. He was just some guy we used to get Adele pregnant."

Her anger grew as she talked with distaste about the young man whom they had gotten drunk several nights in a row to ensure fertilization. They had checked him out in the brains department, of course, and he was smart enough.

While I would readily admit in those days that male-female partnering often lacked a lot of love and understanding, I believed that a parent from each gender seemed the best way to teach a child how to navigate in a two-gender world.

"When is she due?" I quickly asked to fill the silence left by my surprise.

"In January. It will be a great new year."

It was the year we gradually grew apart. They withdrew more and more from the world and I withdrew gradually from them. Not by any specific decision. Simply because it was difficult for me to watch them with their child – born a boy – and know that he would have to grow up living with the anger toward men they spoke of frequently, and it bothered me.

I knew the world had to grow together, not farther apart. Men and women together had to find a way to put aside blame and recrimination and become responsible for caring coupling in a way they had never done before. One gender simply using another person wasn't the answer. But that was the rage then.

The '60s, despite its awakening peace-consciousness and anti-war talk, was still a war zone. It was the first "new age" before the official New Age was born. And it was pulling itself and its values sharply away from the generation it had left behind.

My close friend from New York in the '60s – Rose – and I are still in touch, though in the intervening years she has been married, divorced, moved across the continent, and lived with three or so male partners. During that time, I went up the business ladder in New York, became a yogi and a teacher, donned the turban and white garb of a Sikh, went into business on my own and moved most of the way across the continent.

Despite all that change, we have always shared a deep friendship with each other. Nothing has really changed between us.

Whenever we get together – a trip of only one state's distance now – it's as if the time in between visits has never happened. We meet and it is just like yesterday. She has had two children. I watched them grow up.

She and I have shared pains, joys, hopes and loneliness, and are closer than most any two sisters I have ever known.

Women seek the love of women to gain nurturance that they generally can not find in depth with men. It is a love untarnished by anger over gender or envy of each other. For some, this blossoms into actual partnering to receive nurturance on a continuing basis.

Nowadays being different is more accepted. Fewer and fewer people from other generations and other lifestyles are angered by differences, and those who are different are learning to drop their anger also.

All that remains is to make the spiritual connection and establish love and community on a planet-wide level. That is the responsibility now being taken up by women. It is women who are now rising to become our spiritual leaders for the new millennium.

8

LOVE DIES OR LOVE GROWS

*Those who do not like themselves
and show it to themselves daily,
do not have the ability to truly
like others, let alone love them.*

Love Dies or Love Grows

Consider what happens in that most common situation that women refer to as "love dying."

So much has to do with imagineering – the "imagination engineering" of relationships that we do so well. Based on common language patterns that reveal deeply held beliefs, there appear to be two kinds of love for most women.

First, there is that instant bells-ringing, flashy, star-crossed state known as "falling in love." Rarely does it last long – it is painful and usually quickly undone. Most men move through it faster than women.

When this kind of love dies, it is abrupt, often leaving the woman feeling she has been "jilted." Both sides in this type of affair may feel themselves to be star-crossed lovers, karmically connected, linked by destiny, and all those popular phrases. *Romeo and Juliet* are a typical example.

In fact, infatuation is such a compulsive force in this type of relationship that no one even conceives of the love-state "growing" – simply lasting forever. As if anything in life could exist without change!

"I want her to remain exactly the way she is today (when I marry her)" is the man's wish. Meanwhile, the woman has the perennial desire to somehow change him. Of course, she also wants all the exciting things she sees in him to remain frozen in time.

What happens when "love dies?"

"She isn't the same woman I married," the man quickly laments.

The woman feels the man sold her a bill of goods. She feels used.

What really happened? Was it a case of mistaken identity? Hardly. It was the often-conscious act of imagination engineering at work. They were courting each other, displaying the sweetest looking aspects of their personality to win each other's favor. Have you ever seen birds courting, displaying their brightest feathers, and fluffing themselves up to look big and important? It's not much different.

The human would-be partners displayed themselves with "false colors," and sold their personality.

The personality is simply not permanent, nor does it ever seem stable. It changes almost from moment to moment, as if the person is a chameleon. It does not possess the permanency of the soul. Most people marry or partner with a personality, only to be disappointed, even frightened, when it changes.

If you don't see the distinction, ask yourself this: does the soul get depressed or the personality?

A hundred things every day affect our moods, feelings, commotional emotions, and we blow with the wind of those changes. To be in love with something that fluctuates so much is dangerous. Yet that is exactly the nature and degree of attachment so many people have to this thing called love.

It is the ultimate roller coaster and the ride is far from a joy ride.

This in-love business happens because of early and repeated inoculations. Both genders grow up being programmed to believe they have to hear bells ringing for it to be the "right person." Many members of the generation that grew up singing the popular song, "True Love," are still searching for it.

This "in-love" state is often mistaken for the deeper state known as "loving." Unfortunately, for most people getting to this state often requires surviving the "in love" state.

By contrast, "loving" builds slowly over time and rarely ends quickly. Love hardly ever arrives with bells ringing and it does not go out with a bang.

Love arrives often when you're not looking, when you're not trying to find the "right" man or woman. In fact, it often happens when you've dropped the word "right" and are just enjoying a friendship.

That friendship may evolve into loving over a period of months, or even years, before it dawns on both people that something very beautiful has happened in their lives and they want to commit to continue growing it.

For a true loving state to "die," it has to be eroded over time, through negligence, miscommunication, declining partnering skills or major shifts in the growth rate of either partner.

Why? Because love once built can weather many storms. And even if the relationship cannot continue as active intimate partnering, in some way the feeling of love never dies. It is a deep soul-level commitment that undoubtedly reflects prior lifetimes of involvement.

DEATH BY CHOCOLATE

Loving dies because all too often we look at love as something that we have to have to fix our lives. That's treating love something like a fix, not much different than a drug or chocolate.

We the lovers have to be fixed. Love is a miracle fixer.

We apply to the love state words such as saved - "he saved me from a lonely life" - and the word broken - "he broke my heart," for example.

What that all boils down to is a sell-out. To believe that anything outside you can save or break you is a sellout and the worst kind of imagineering. Every time a woman uses those words she is disempowering herself and over-empowering the man. She is putting him in charge of her life. Her emotional tank is running on empty, forever needing to be filled up by someone else.

It also puts the woman in an irreversible situation. A broken heart that cannot be healed. Patched up perhaps, but not healed.

Few men ever use such language regarding the heart. However, when a woman says it - the power of her words being so strong - the man reluctantly buys into the finality of her broken heart.

What can you do to avoid such an impasse?

Women, your power lies inside you. Don't give it away. Don't even believe you can. Don't ever believe that something is irreversible. That's giving up. That's surrendering. You've beaten yourself.

As powerless as you think you may be, your heart will never leave you. You have to pretend very very hard to convince people you have no heart. As powerful as you are, you cannot actually give away your heart. Put a curtain of steel around that burning light, and still the light does not go out.

Believe it. Now, how will you live knowing this is true? Knowing you don't need a man to rescue you? How will you live?

Decide, first, to live with yourself as number one in importance to you.

If you did that, would that mean you'd not be supportive of your husband? Of course not. That you'd somehow be derelict in your duty to your children? No.

It would mean that you'd take care of your needs and wants each day. That you would not put some basic self-needs aside in order to serve others and let them run your life until you collapse with fatigue and resentment for all they took from you.

"I gave you the best years of my life," remember that line?

Taking care of yourself first doesn't have to take a lot of time, and it does help you be stronger and more able to be there for all the others you love.

And what about the worst accusation of all – would putting yourself first mean you'd be selfish?

People who think that way buy into the old belief that human love is a limited commodity and that what one person gets directly leads to someone else's loss. In other words, caring for yourself is somehow denying caring to others who need it. This is one of the most insidious guilt trips we use to destroy ourselves. Don't take the trip.

We have to build our inner territory every day. Self-caring is the basis for renewing ourselves. With it, our love for others can continue to grow uninterrupted and be continually demonstrated.

Those women who are blessed as to produce harmonious, loving families do so because they know how to continue to grow harmony inside themselves. They are able to bless others because they know inside themselves that they are blessed.

There are thousands of examples of this I have seen over the years.

Lily is a woman in her forties, married to a well-known lawyer. They have three teenage sons. She grew up in France, the only daughter of a father who wanted boys and instead got her and only her.

"He never left me alone," she said the first time I met her, "and Jacob is just like him." She drew a painful analogy between her dead father and living husband.

"Even my boys are always criticizing me, hanging on me and demanding I do everything for them and then it's never good enough."

She had been fighting a lonely battle against male dominance for more than forty years. It seemed there was never any time free just for her. She was always engaged in battle. Battle to force them to do things her way and thus gain their support.

"What would getting their support do for you?" I asked.

"Well for one thing I'd have their respect. Maybe then they'd love me."

"What would you think if I told you that you might already have their love and support and respect but that, by trying to force them to do things your way, you might be jeopardizing all that?"

For a brief second she looked stunned, then her face broke out into laughter. "I'd say you were joking with me."

"No, really, let's say that's possible."

"But it's not possible. Their actions prove otherwise. They refuse to let me do anything my way. They have no respect for me."

I decided to give her an example both of her power and their love and respect for her. I chose a manner that would also build her inner power. Since she was the only woman in her household, it was obvious that she was the focal point of their attention. But, since she kept making aggressive forays into their territory, demanding things of them, they did the male response and made counter-forays into her territory.

"Let me give you a simple test of the power you think you don't have over them. Are you willing to try something new?"

She nodded her head yes.

"You just learned a new meditation here today. How about doing it for 11 minutes twice a day every day at home?"

She laughed again. "How? Where? I can't even lie down in my own bedroom without one of them bursting in to ask me some dumb question."

"I see the problem. You have no territory. You need to assign some to yourself."

"What do you mean by that?"

"I mean that you keep a great house with room in it for everyone to have their own special place except you've left no room in it for yourself. Let's use this little meditation to start to give you space, okay?"

"Sure."

I outlined for her some simple steps to take over the next week. First, she was to explain to her husband and sons that she was doing something to help herself relax and improve her health. She needed their help to do this. She was going to do a meditation twice a day for twenty minutes – this would give her time to rest briefly after the actual meditation – and she needed to be alone in her room undisturbed except for true emergencies. She got their agreement to support her in this.

Two days later she was on the phone angry with me. One of her boys had burst into the room during her meditation. He'd broken the agreement. I explained to her that she needed to repeat and define the request better – spelling out what was an emergency – and getting new agreement on that among all her men. Then, she should put a note on the bedroom door when she was meditating.

A week later I saw her in my office. Her response was tentative at first.

"Well, no one's interrupted me...yet," she began.

"Good," I jumped in to fend off any negativity. "And how do you feel with time off to yourself?"

"Actually I don't know. It's all so new."

"And you're getting your way and they're helping you get your way, right?"

"Well I wouldn't go so far as to say that," she replied rather testily.

"Okay, then it's time we took our little experiment a step or so farther. How would you like to have some more time off, just to rest, not to do anything at all?"

"They'll never agree to that."

"Yes they will, if you thank them each time they help you take that time off."

"What do you mean, thank them?"

"People and puppies are sometimes very much alike – they like to be rewarded for good behavior, even if you think that good behavior is merely the absence of bad behavior."

After a little more instruction, she went home and for a week, took two additional twenty-minute breaks in her room each day. When she came in a week later she was actually quite excited.

With some more understanding and coaching, she actually managed to turn a small spare room into a meditation room where she was able to take time out for long periods with the full support of her family.

It was an important part of her regaining her own inner power, a place for herself in her home, and a recognition that if she avoided confrontation she could enjoy their support and love without ever having to engage in battle.

She discovered that instead of fighting them she had really been fighting herself.

You have to have the courage to care for yourself. I say courage because you have to face your fear that you may lose someone else's love while they wait around for you to complete caring for yourself.

But that is the only route by which you will reclaim and live your innate divinity. In doing so, you will receive infinite love and become infinitely loving.

I have seen this process happen in countless women. Family women. Business women. They start what they call "sadhana" which means simply daily spiritual practice.

It can make a difference in even the most extreme cases where love is at risk. It is the greatest difference between a life without love for self and a life with love for self and God.

THE KILLING FIELD

Nothing kills love more completely than rage.

A woman must be able to contain her man, to keep him at peace. When she does, and he experiences that peace over time, he will cover her. He becomes her defender, protecting her from all that is outside her peaceful environment.

If she cannot contain him, turn him from his dark side and his rage, she must leave him. His rage, unbridled, will defeat her grace, her peace and excellence.

No matter how well-intentioned any woman may be, there comes a time when she may have to recognize that she cannot overlook some things. Abuse turned to rage can kill, directly and indirectly. Why do you think those who are enraged often kill their own loved ones in their family?

Rage also kills psychologically. The one who rages kills hope, happiness, and over time deteriorates the health of those around them. Rage cuts through the energy fields just like a knife.

First rage accelerates stress everywhere. Shouting shrivels the auras of everyone nearby. Judgement and criticism of everyone becomes abundant, and responsibility non-existent. Blame is placed on others for personal failures, leaving no way out and no options other than the fast road downhill.

Can rage be stopped? Yes, for a while. But the person generating the rage has to stop himself. That's the only permanent fix. Otherwise, at some point, if the woman tries to stop it, she will be run over by that rage just as surely as if she were a victim of road rage.

"We were driving down the road at eighty miles an hour and he was screaming at the top of his lungs, screaming at me and at our son that we were driving him crazy. And we hadn't said a thing. Nothing."

The woman sitting in front of me is in tears. She thought she and her husband and son were enjoying a pleasant weekend in the country. She knew he had brought work along with him but he always did that.

She wasn't prepared for him to throw his computer across the room, curse his loved ones and blame them for keeping him from doing his work. In shock, she had watched him throw all their belongings into their car and drive like a madman back to town in the middle of the night.

"Did he finally calm down?" I asked.

"No. He just got quiet, said something about maybe he shouldn't be around us. Then he dropped us off at the house and drove downtown to work all night at his office."

"Perhaps he was right."

"To go to work?"

"No. Perhaps he should be apart from you for awhile."

She looked at me with a mixture of hurt and surprise. "But you know I'm important to him keeping himself together. We've talked a lot about that."

"Yes, we have. Let me ask you, when was the last time you meditated in the morning like you love to do, say for three or four days in a row?"

She looked down, avoiding my eyes. "A long time, months I guess."

"What's stopping you?"

"I stay up late at night with him, cuddling on the couch, trying to make things happier for him. Then I'm just too tired in the morning to get up early."

She was leaving herself unprotected, weakened, and telling herself it was for him. "That's a poor trade-off, don't you think?"

"What do you mean?"

"You're trading off a practice that, by your own words, makes you strong in order to try to make him happier, and it isn't working. Right?"

"I guess not."

"So where do you want to go from here?"

"I don't know."

"Yes you do. Do you want to be weak or strong?"

"Strong, of course." Her eyes glared at me with near-defiance.

"Then you start by resuming your morning meditations. Whether or not he is there with you."

"But what about when he comes home late at night. Shouldn't I stay up with him?"

"Tell him you're going to resume going to bed at a decent hour. Leave him with a cup of tea or something, and go to bed. You have to be number one for you. That way you will see clearly what you have to do and when you have to do it."

She left my office a bit miffed, knowing that I had told her what she already knew but had avoided doing. I wondered how long it would take until I saw her again. Actually, she called first before she came in. He had left her, just walked out.

"I couldn't stop him," she blurted out between tears. "Where will he go, what will he do?"

"You may not know the answers to any of that. And, then again, he may come back. You can't tell. Keep doing your morning meditations and keep getting stronger. You have yourself and your son to keep together."

She screwed her face up, a question coming into focus. "Is there ever a light at the end of the tunnel? Is there an end to the tunnel?" she asked me.

"Yes," I replied. "There is a light and an end of the tunnel. But then there is another tunnel, and a tunnel after that. We get stronger and they get more challenging. They keep coming one after another, until the time when we stop looking for the light at the end of the tunnel and we realize that the light was always in the tunnel. The light is in us. We just have to look up to the third eye when we meditate and see what is really there, the way Home. We have to find the light inside, hold on to it, and turn the power up. Then there are no more tunnels."

She decided to wait for him and take no action other than to continue doing her meditations. She could have written him off – many women would. But she did not.

I knew he had to burn out his anger. If not, it would burn him out. He had reached a point where love had to die or grow, and first he had to grow. It took him six months until he called her.

"He said he hit a stumbling block and he knew he didn't want to go on alone without me, me and our son," she said to me on the phone, her voice full of tears and hope.

"Do you want him back with you still?" I asked.

"Yes. He says his rage is over now."

"Over for now. You will have to see how well he can contain himself."

"I love him."

"Yes, I know you do."

"And he loves me."

"That was not in question. Now he will have to learn to love himself."

"I will help him."

Over the months that followed he began a new chapter in his life. He started to rise early with her and meditate. At first he fell asleep by the time the third meditation started. But then, gradually, he found he enjoyed doing this practice with her.

It has been a year now. He still occasionally gets angry. But they are still meditating together.

He turned a stumbling block into a building block. Actually, they did it together.

BUILDING BLOCKS, STUMBLING BLOCKS

On the Soul's path, which many call our spiritual path, there are building blocks and there are stumbling blocks.

As we deal with these, we travel through various stages of consciousness. We move from awareness of our unit self, to awareness of a partner, to friends and community, then on to our connection to all things and an awareness of ourselves at one with the Great Soul.

"The light is within all the Beings and all the Beings are within the light," wrote a great Eastern teacher in the 16th century.

Our journey in Human form was chosen for us to learn how to live in the continual consciousness of ourselves in that Light State where there is no separation from Source. For it is in feeling our separation from Great Soul that we doom ourselves to endless loneliness over endless lifetimes.

No one feels this loneliness, this separation and abandonment, more than women.

By seeking to bring new life into this world, each woman hopes to bridge this loneliness. In seeking earthly partnership, she reignites the memory carried deep in cellular memory of the Divine Partner. It is in filling herself with earthly love that she hopes to recapture a sense of that infinite love that feeds all souls.

No food is as filling as that food. Yet throughout her lifetime - powered by that loneliness, the fear of abandonment and the need for acceptance and comfort - she will attempt to feed herself with many limited foods. Some are destructive - alcohol, drugs, food itself in quantity. She can become driven, obsessive, compulsed into meaningless partnerships.

Partnership for most women is a place of countless stumbling blocks, and yet a place for boundless hope and learning.

One such stumbling block for a woman comes tied to a terrible lie – that finding and marrying a man will solve all her problems. It's the worst trap.

Countless mothers have taught their daughters to snatch up budding doctors and lawyers to ensure their future. It's a gross extension of the white knight syndrome.

Try to find a rescuer and you are eternally lost.

At every Womanheart Retreat, we ask the participants to form a group to rewrite women's history. The history they rewrite is the story of Cinderella. Each retreat gives us yet a new twist on the liberated Cinderella.

Couched in humor and song, the story is changed by each group in their own unique interpretations. The results reflect a woman's new-found sense of freedom, her loss of neediness, her decision to be a queen without needing a king to crown her. In the process, each Cinderella reforms her wicked stepmother and stepsisters.

She may or may not accept the Prince in her life, but it is on her own terms.

"I thought he was the answer to my dreams when he married me," she said, her eyes misting over fleetingly with the faint but beautiful memory of the wedding day. "I never dreamed how horrible he would become."

Margie was telling me of the fairytale marriage she thought she had when she married John five years earlier, only to discover that he had been cheating behind her back with several women, beginning about a year after their wedding.

"He might as well have dumped me at the altar," she said defiantly. "Our marriage meant nothing to him."

It didn't take long for me to discover what had happened between them. Margie had wedded and been bedded by him and then let down her hair, her air of mystery, and her desire to serve him the customary cup of coffee when he came home each night. She had taken him for granted. She had married him just to be married. John had done the same thing.

They never grew to know and love each other. They were only living figureheads to each other.

You can spot it in the language couples often use – "the little wife" (even though she may have gained forty pounds!), or "my good husband" (but she hasn't seen him do anything good for her in months!), and so forth. People relate to each other as titles, not as individuals.

So John was fair game for every doe-eyed woman who smiled at him. It happens all the time.

And was he remorseful? Not really. Of course this wasn't the role a "good husband" should play. So, when his wife found out, he was appropriately contrite, begging forgiveness. Yes, he was sincerely afraid of losing his wife, but also equally afraid of what his girlfriend would think of him. Perhaps she would think he had deserted her. That wasn't an image he wanted to live with either.

So he was trapped. Trapped between two conflicting roles. He wanted to please them both.

The marriage survived and continued. John's last girlfriend found another John and eventually married him.

Did everyone live happily ever after? Hardly. John and Margie try to keep up appearances for themselves that they are still being "the good husband" (even if he can't forget the other women) and "the good wife" (even if she can't forgive him).

If she could have forgiven him and used that to draw him into a higher state of love, things might have been different.

FORGIVENESS IS DIVINE AND HUMAN

Forgiveness needs to become human, not just something we expect of the Divine.

One major stumbling block in partnership is holding on to grief. It keeps people from growing together. Oddly enough, even after divorce a woman can regret that she did not offer forgiveness. But still she holds on to her unforgiving position.

A young woman who was a former client called me in the early hours one morning with a curious story she wanted me to unravel for her.

She had been driving the night before and a voice spoke in her ear, "Do you forgive me?" it asked. She recognized the voice of her ex-husband. They had been divorced for ten years.

Without a thought, she answered, speaking out loud. "No, I guess I don't forgive you. You promised things and never delivered them."

She explained to me that this was an issue she had with him and with other men since then. But she was surprised by her answer because she thought she had forgiven him long ago. She resolved to call him the next day and talk about it.

She was too late. The next morning she received a phone call and was told that the day before her ex-

husband had fallen, hit his head and died. She asked me what this all meant.

"It was a message from the departing soul, a message and a parting opportunity for you," I told her.

Of course she didn't understand.

"This is an issue you've dealt with all your life. He came to see if you had let that go. That would be one less impediment to him moving on, one less thing holding him back."

"But I thought I had."

"Obviously not. You didn't get the point. When somebody doesn't do what they promise for someone, it's not about the other person – about you – it's about them. That's their problem."

"So I wasn't part of the problem?"

"Not part of his problem. Your problem was different. Yours was about letting go, about not holding others to blame for what they can't do for you. You personalized what he didn't do, thinking that was a personal statement from him to you. It was a statement from him about him."

"Then why do others continue to let me down?"

"Because you draw people to you who do this, over and over, so you can learn your lesson, the lesson of not taking things personally and letting go."

"So how do I forgive him?"

"By letting him go this final time. Praying for his release and helping to send him on."

I gave her a meditation that does just that – helps the soul to rise. She had to chant it before 5 in the morning, for 11 minutes for a total of 17 days. It is an ancient formula from the yogis that has helped release countless souls from the earthly realm.

She did it at first reluctantly, but she did not miss one day. She felt considerably more peaceful after that.

Forgiveness is a cardinal issue with most of us, especially women. How many times have you found yourself holding on to some little incident that seemed to be an insult, unable to let it go for days, weeks, even years?

One client came to me incensed that her neighbor wanted permission to build the first part of his new front walkway twelve inches over onto her property line. The plan threatened nothing of her vegetation or the look of her front lawn – points she readily admitted.

There was plenty of space for this to be done. But she saw it as a pattern of abuse by him against her property and her person.

Why? Five years earlier he had inadvertently trimmed one of her bushes back when he trimmed his own – an oversight for which he promptly apologized when she confronted him.

He even brought her flowers. And, in a further attempt to please her, he planted a companion dogwood bush on her side of the property line to match the one he planted on his own side. She was shocked and in no way saw it as a present. She had it ripped out.

She had never forgiven him all those years since. Now when he wanted to do something else, her response was a shrill "How dare he!"

She was unable to let her anger go and so the neighbor, a bit puzzled, moved the start of his pathway back twelve inches.

Had she been able to de-intensify herself, she would have seen that her anger was far greater than the situation warranted. In fact, it was a perfect opportunity to learn what battles are worth fighting. Clearly, we cannot fight every one.

His intention was not to do harm, even though he did do harm. Most likely, he was thoughtlessly trimming bushes while thinking of the next day's activities at work. Men often do things when they are not "all present and accounted for". That is their way.

He even tried to make it up to her – kind of like the husband who doesn't think an apology is enough so he brings home an apple pie for his wife who promptly accuses him of sabotaging her diet. She did not even see the intended apology in his gift.

Because he did not apologize the way she wanted, he was forever wrong.

What is this thing called forgiveness? Is it truly only a quality of the Divine, as the bard wrote, and we as humans can only err?

Consider the roots of the word "human." It comes from the Sanskrit words "hu" and "man" which translates as "the light of the soul." Remember that meaning when you find yourself asking someone to forgive you, saying, "I am only human," as if human were the miserable, wretched polarity of the Divine.

In reality, being human is being Divine. When you live in this state, you accept all things and all people as they are. You do not judge them, you simply see them. From that point forward, you will learn the most from those you know and meet.

How is that possible? Take yourself – your hurts, your sense of territory – out of the equation. At the same time that you are a participant in some situation, be also an observer.

Just as I mentioned to the lady who heard the voice of her ex-husband asking if she had forgiven him, learn to distinguish between your lesson and the lesson the other person is learning.

Consider the neighbor who trimmed the wrong bush. What was his intent? Was he actually "all there" when he did the foul deed? Obviously not. So is it better to punish him for what he unwittingly did, or let that go and try to spark some greater degree of awareness and responsibility in him?

Perhaps when she rebuked him for his initial mistake, he already woke up. After all, he tried to make amends. And this time he was politely requesting permission to take up twelve inches of her territory when he might otherwise have gone ahead with the plan believing she would never notice.

So his honest request could well have been met with gratitude and a thank you. He had learned a lesson.

Would you not so reward a child who learned? Would you not so wish to have someone treat you this way? Do you not understand that God also acknowledges and rewards those who include thank you in their prayers?

Why? Because even the Great Source needs to hear that you have learned lessons. Then you are ready to receive more, some of which you may even begin to see are truly gifts.

One of the reasons you do not always get a "yes" response to your prayer requests is that you pray like a needy person. Ask for what you require, not "I need this" or "I want that". God did not make us needy people, but divine beings! Look at all that comes to you as a gift and the lessons will be swift and painless.

It is in resisting lessons that we create stumbling blocks. In accepting all that is, as it is, we turn these into building blocks, and life becomes a series of gifts.

So what do we actually have to forgive? Who has sinned against us?

Consider this possibility: *All that has happened to you, all that is happening now and will happen to you, is making you great. So can you not be grateful?*

Gratitude is a continual expression of someone who creates building blocks. Gratitude will get you everything. Judgement and punishing responses will leave you lonely and feeling battered.

SEE THE FAULTS AND CHOSE TO UNSEE THEM

There is a certain wisdom in forgiveness. There is an even greater wisdom in the words of a prayer I recite every morning. It goes: *"Allow me to see the faults of others, and chose to unsee them."*

In some ways it is more difficult than forgiveness. Yet it is far simpler.

As I mentioned earlier, what if all that happens is part of God's plan? What if all that doesn't happen is part of that plan also?

Then no one has acted to do anything wrong to you. They are doing their part.

That doesn't mean you have to excuse everything that everyone does in your presence. It means: accept it as a gift. Learn and grow from it. And be grateful to the person for the lesson.

See the fault and unsee it. Bless him or her. Don't react and get hooked into the emotionality of the experience. If you don't get hooked and react, there's a good chance you will see what is the best response to what has happened.

Maybe that means to give help in some new way. Or maybe it means to back off and give someone time and space to grow.

Love can die when you stay too long in a bad situation. Love can also grow at a distance. Love is not defined by your proximity to someone. Some situations are like prickly pear cactus – you must love them without hugging them!

See the fault, chose to unsee it. From that place of neutrality allow a new kind of knowingness to happen. The next step will come to you.

Do this and your life will no longer be driven by anyone other than the Divine. The Divine in You.

Hallelujah, sister! Saat Naam and Amen.

9

BECOMING THE NOBLE WOMAN

*If you learn to see your life
as a series of victories – even miracles –
then you build your belief in yourself.*

*You come to trust yourself
and like yourself.*

Becoming The Noble Woman

If there is one command each woman should hear every day when she arises – and several times during the day – it is: "Never surrender!"

Why? Because you lose the game of life every time you give in. And I don't mean give in to your children and your mates.

Far more importantly, you lose your life when you give in to your fears, your tears and doubts – to all the mental garbage you know so well how to generate, just as your mother did before you and her mother did before her.

Why do you think men don't trust you? Don't you realize they fear you? In just a fraction of a second, you can have one thought which – by the look that thought produces on your face and the few words you may say – will destroy their day.

 Never surrender to your doubts, your fears, your tears. Don't let the mind and its catacombs of envisioned/remembered worries and hells take over. Never surrender!

You are who you tell yourself you are. You are who you live your life as. You are who you believe you are. One thought can destroy your day. Repeated often enough, one thought can destroy your life. Don't let it in!

 Every moment you create your own reality. Choose a reality of virtues and light. Say "No!" to the negative thoughts. Say "No!" to no.

You can create an environment around you that will elevate others. You can become worthy of worship and praise.

Is this a control game? You bet it is. It's got a simple title: "Who's in charge here?" You or your mind. Now translate "you" into "Your soul."

CREATING SACRED SPACE

Living with your soul demands that you create sacred space around you.

You can only do that when you take charge of your life. You can only do that when you can create sacred space within you.

Some of you may think you know what that means and even know how to create sacred space. Don't be so certain. You have to be taught, taught well, and then you have to practice it over and over, in dozens of different ways every day of your life. In addition, you have to be trained to be alert to all the ways you deteriorate yourself and your sacred space.

If you are an adult Western woman, you are probably the least knowledgeable about sacred space of any creature on the planet.

What is sacred space? In its simplest form, it is that space within you that is your touchstone to the Divine. It can be reached through meditation or prayer. It allows you to feel elevated even in dark situations. It is your personal resource available at all times.

Those who have it re-create it around them.

You live in a place called a house. What makes it a home? Your presence. Your peaceful presence as a woman. There may be rooms for all who live with you, but is there a special place for you?

So many women have no place for themselves in their own home. You need a place to go to be quiet - not the bedroom. There you are mostly unconscious. Maybe you can't afford much space, so "your place" will have to be a special chair with a small table where you can put a vase and flowers.

The flowers will remind you every day how special you are.

Then you need to spend time there, to meditate, pray, go inside yourself and listen to the answers within.

That is how you nurture sacred space within. It is also how you become a nurturer of others, whether or not you are ever a biologic mother to children.

Any baby who could speak would tell you what sacred space is: it is called Mother. Mother equals safe frequency. It was the only frequency baby knew in the womb and hopefully it was peaceful and loving. That was where baby learned whether or not it was wanted in this world and whether or not this would be a safe world.

Then, when baby came out, it found there were other frequencies - most of them not so safe even if simply because they were different than the mother frequency it knew. Only a few babies are fully protected by knowing parents who keep baby safe within the nine-foot-wide shelter of the mother's aura for the first 40 days until it can develop its own auric protection.

Then later, when the baby has developed its own aura, it only takes one little upsetting dream to send the child crying back into its mother's arms. For psychological consolation, you think? No, for sacred space. For some desire to suckle on the nipple again? Oh you people, captured by the mind! No, for sacred space.

Children try to crawl, ingratiate and win their way back into that sacred space for years.

Your pet cat and dog hang close to you because you can generate sacred space. Friends, business associates, near and distant family members want to spend time with you because of it. Did you think it was because of your wit or wisdom? Ask them.

The ones who are dearest and who love you the most will say, after all the rationalizations are aside, something like, "I just like being near you." Or maybe some other such wording as, "It's nice hanging out together."

That's a deep recognition of sacred space.

You create your sacred space and it's called your "presence." And it is the best part of you, the part that really works – not your wit or your wisdom, not even your heart. Why not? Because heart without an effective presence around you leaves you open and vulnerable. Just as wisdom and wit, without heart, leave you cold and uncompassionate and not emotionally trustworthy.

To create sacred space is to engage in a process of self-mastery. When is it complete? Never. Each day you complete it when you can go to bed feeling cozy and special with your Self and your God. And those "plus days" accumulate, like so much wealth in a bank account. After awhile you can have a bad day and draw out some of that accumulated wealth to cover you during that hard time. But you must continue building it every day.

When do you achieve full mastery? You might as well ask: When can you be absolutely safe from your fears, your hells, your angers, your childhood hurts, your raging husband, and your whiney kids? When you die, your degree of mastery will be judged by where your last thought was. That will tell whether you are Earth-bound again – to follow the continuing course in mastery – or whether your thought of oneness with God takes you home.

Sacred space is about safety. It is about staying centered, being focused, staying with any one intention you have, committing to it, putting the plan together and carrying it off until you have reached your goal. When you can do all that, you have achieved and maintained sacred space, at least for that period of time and action.

Remember earlier when I said the prayers of women sustain the Earth? Did you not wonder why I didn't speak about the prayers of men?

When it comes to prayers, didn't God create a democracy? Yes, true. Everybody's prayers count, men and women. But women's count more. Just as women's tears and anger hurt more.

Women are the creators of sacred space and every action you take, every thought you think impacts that space, builds it or destroys it.

So what are men supposed to do, what is their role?

You create the harmonious environment they relate to as the nest, and then they protect it and you within it. If you pollute the nest – or allow it to be polluted – with worries, fears and arguments, they will not protect it. They will go elsewhere.

The home you build together is your product, just like a child. You make it sacred. This Earth is your child. Each woman contributes to making it sacred.

Look at the opposite scenario. When women create wars – at home or globally – nothing is left. Women make war in a far more devastating fashion than men could ever conceive.

Don't blame a man for destroying the nest. The woman allowed it to happen. Not consciously, but indeed it was the woman who failed to maintain sacred space, either through ignorance or letting herself down in her own sacred space.

How can this happen? We have been raised ignorant of how to create and maintain sacred space. We have been told – and bought hook, line and sinker – the myth that we need a man to build a nest. We have been given program after program that supports our needing the man to create and maintain that nest as well as protect it.

Often the man tries to do all this while we – in our fear and doubt and criticisms – foul the space with our words and frowns, and then flee in the face of his rage against us. Do you not see that you have destroyed the peace most precious to him?

No one feels that loss more desperately than our children do. Because to them, from the beginning, Mother was God. The only God-frequency they knew.

As the kid grew up, he heard and saw how we destroyed sacred space with our arguments and tears and fears. That's how the kid concluded that God had to be somewhere else, someone else, anywhere where there was sacred space. Or, maybe God was dead and there was no place left to turn.

The kid shouting at his parents in rage, "I don't believe you anymore," isn't making a statement about whether or not you are telling him the truth. In reality he is saying, "I don't trust you anymore." He doesn't feel safe around you.

Those who create sacred space also have the power to destroy it. Either way you will be long remembered.

A NEW ROYALTY

When I was growing up in the 1940s, we used to speak of "women of bearing," women who had "carriage" – expressions that even at that time had lost their meaning to most people except to the few of us who hung out around the fast-dying-out old-wealth class.

These words, and others like them, referred to a timeless nobility. Not nobility "bestowed" by lineage or birth, but a nobility of character earned by deeds. That nobility is ageless and classless.

Today this nobility is truly needed. To be built, it requires hard work and diligent effort, but it is the only hope for humankind – to ensure the survival of the kindness that makes us sublimely human.

We must live in the purity and nobility of our soul and let it grow.

Yet, we ask the question – "How?" over and over.

How can women survive with their fears and self-doubts? How can they survive with men of rage? With men whom they fear and cannot trust? With men who fear them and cannot trust them?

There is only one way. The way of becoming who we truly are: women of courage and love, women who are true to their word, who do not vacillate or trade values or compromise themselves for short-term gains.

If you as a woman live only for love, you will never be worthy of trust.

You think men want someone to love. No, they want to trust you first. After you demonstrate that, they will see if you are worthy of love.

What do they want to trust you for? Loyalty to them, yes, but things much deeper. They want you to be a rock, someone they can depend on when things are tough for them. And, despite the fact that they may promote themselves as strong and capable, every man knows deep inside that he is barely holding his world together. He needs the woman to hold his world together emotionally, to make his home a place of refuge for him.

Such a home, and such a woman, he will protect to the death. She makes his life worth living.

You want a knight in shining armor? First, make yourself worthy of one. Make yourself noble with your words, your quiet strength, your belief in his goodness. Through him, commit to a Higher Partner that protects you even when times are rough between you and your earthly partner.

First make yourself a queen, but not one who dictates and rules – not a naughty princess who wields power like a sword and competes with her mate for the throne.

A true queen beautifies the castle, spreads smiles and a voice of music and friendly words through each room, and never, never lets any one see her "losing it."

Let me tell you a true story about such a queen.

There was a great queen once who was truly the model of human victory, not by conquest of the world but conquest over herself. She was respected by all, even her enemies.

Even today, all these generations later, she is still revered as being calm under stress, unflappable, never falling apart even under the severest threat to her ships or her country. She ruled with peace and justice.

No one knew, not even her most private of servants, that late at night when all were asleep, she would go into her most private closet and there, and only there, cry and holler and shout out her angers and fears. And then only for a few moments. After that, she would either sleep, or emerge with a calm smile on her face.

Was her smile a lie? No. Her truth was her victory over the turmoil inside. The face of her victory was what she shared with others – not the face of her fury. She could have freaked out but she chose to keep the freak in.

Each woman has within her the same indomitable spirit.

Yogi Bhajan has often taught that the old yogic texts say that each woman has within her all the elements of the entire universe. She was given this power because it is her gift to be able to recreate the universe wherever she goes – a universe of calm or one of chaos.

Which universe she creates depends entirely on what she creates inside herself.

Let's say you're angry and you think I'm asking you to smile and hide the anger. Does that mean I'm asking you to lie to everyone else because the truth is you're not smiling inside?

Who made your truth inside? You. You bought into the anger and you built it. Well, you can buy out of it and choose another way.

DROPPING A HABIT

The more you focus on your pain the bigger it gets, even if you think that focus will somehow help you understand it or control it. Look at it as if you want to drop an unhealthy habit, such as smoking.

You must know that trying to stop smoking is one sure way to defeat achieving that goal. Because the more you think about stopping smoking, the more you focus on smoking. That makes it larger than life and helps it have a powerful hold on you.

The only lasting way to drop a habit is to replace it with another habit that you can focus on and build to be even stronger than the first one.

In my thirties, when I was still a harried business executive trudging the canyons of New York, I had a four-pack-a-day cigarette habit – which is to say the habit had me. Once when I tried to cut back on my habit, I quickly found that all that concentration on smoking worked briefly, but then only allowed me to watch it build right back up again.

Kind of like "watching your waistline" – you can watch it go either down or up.

Then I got into yoga and meditation and, most importantly for my habit, into specialized yoga-style breathing. In fact, I really got hooked on breathing and how great I felt after I did even a few minutes of it.

Then, one morning when I had been out late at a party smoking far too much – it seems to go along with talking and dancing – I got up to do my regular morning routine of fifteen minutes of yoga and yogic breathing.

The minute I started the special breaths, my throat felt as if it were on fire. What a shock! I walked over to my purse, took out the cigarettes and lighter, and threw them away. There simply wasn't a choice. It was either stop this breathing that was making me feel so great, or stop smoking.

So you see, I never really gave up smoking – I simply took up breathing.

Dropping a negative emotion is not very different from dropping a smoking habit. *Don't try to give up your emotional pain – take up smiling and thinking and doing good things with yourself.*

You are who you believe you are. You are who you make yourself to be. If you continually tell yourself how good you are and how grateful you are for the good things in your life, your frowns will fade into smiles. This is a "makeover" in a far deeper sense than any makeup artist could ever imagine.

Of course it's not easy. It takes work and diligence. But you can begin any time. Awareness is the first step, and then you need some training.

That's why I started teaching Womanheart retreats and seminars, to give women the training and the tools. That is really what this book is all about.

Everything that's come up to this point that you've read has been one side of the coin – the way most women are today. But that doesn't mean we can't change and grow. I did. And if I did, anybody can. And if anybody can, that includes you!

And the rewards are awesome. Self-respect – that's far more important than self-confidence; the respect of others; and the possibility that the gentle winds of the universe will send you a man who is longing to show some woman his "real self." Because underneath all the rage and difficulty some see in him is truly the heart of a knight in shining armor.

Make yourself a queen. Don't claim the title, just be giving and supportive to those around you – everyone in your "kingdom" so to speak – and the right man just might come along and crown you as his queen. Only when a man can do that does he earn the right to be a king. So he will turn himself into your king, and protect you and honor you.

After that what do you do? Keep on thinking and behaving like that queen and no other woman will ever catch his eye. He will do his best to honor you.

Too good to be true, you say? Well it does happen at times. Haven't you ever wondered how sometimes the nicest looking guys are faithfully married to the homeliest-looking women and they never stray, never spend long nights out with the other guys at a bar, and always seem happy to go home?

You might have wondered, "What does she have that I haven't got?"

Simple. She knows how to be his queen. Not his chick or babe. He puts her on a pedestal because each day she earns it. Only when a man meets, recognizes and matches himself with a true queen and he puts her on a pedestal does he earn the right to put himself on a king pedestal.

That is truly a noble woman – a woman who earns it day after day after day, and lets her king recognize her. How could he be otherwise than kind and good-natured and loving? She sets the example and he basks in that example, seeking to reflect back the same image to her.

The king comes home from the office because his good queen continually reinforces his role as the good king, with her actions and her words. Just as he does for her.

There is a simple human principle of association that makes this happen.

Notice this: the vast majority of people try to be like or similar to those they hang out with. Why? They want to be accepted. Being different gets you rejected. Most youngsters figure out pretty early that if you want someone to like you, you do your best to behave like them. So if you hang out with someone kind, you strive to be kind too.

What about the opposite, is that true also? Of course it is! That's the basic psychology underlying gang development. You know the expression; "If you hang out with the turkeys..." Surely the world has enough turkeys. We don't need any more.

You always have your choice, of course, but beware: the turkeys lose their heads in the end.

LEARNING TO LIKE YOURSELF

A noble woman is always victorious. She is a winner. That means, she wins out over herself, her frailties and discomforts, her fears and misfortunes.

Rethink what you call success and failure. Remove the words right and wrong from the definition. Consider this instead: failure may only be giving up, letting yourself down, not keeping up. Success may simply be keeping up, staying alert and cheerful. On a lot of days that might take a miracle, you say? Maybe there are more miracles in your life than you think.

Now some people think that miracles are only very big things – things that happened far back in history to people called saints.

Let me differ. From all I've seen, miracles are continuing to happen. In fact miracles happen every day to some very ordinary-seeming people – miracles of healing, of faith and hope, miracles of kindness. For some people, there are days when just getting out of bed is a downright miracle.

How do people perform miracles, win out against great odds and survive depressing situations? They never give up.

If you learn to see your life as a series of victories – even miracles – then you build your belief in yourself. You come to trust yourself and like yourself.

The key likes you. Most people innocently ask others to like and love them, when in reality they do not even like themselves.

If you do not like yourself, you will fail yourself every time, and that means you will fail others too. Just like any other self-fulfilling prophecy – you believe you will make mistakes, be undependable, and so your mind is conditioned to let yourself down countless times.

I'm going to start you off right here and now with a few mental short cuts to the liking-yourself process.

COUNTING YOUR VICTORIES MEDITATION

Here's one tool for starting the process – it's called "Counting Your Victories."

Sit down quietly away from disturbances. Close your eyes and take a few long deep breaths. Now focus on something that you did well. Please throw out the word "right" as it is someone else's idea you had to swallow and not your own. If you somehow can't allow yourself to come up with an example of something you did well, then at least look for something you didn't do badly.

This is a form of meditation, so you will want it to be as alive and vibrant a re-experience as possible.

Make a picture of yourself doing this thing well. Hear what was happening then, and even let yourself feel what you were feeling then as you were doing it. Focus and meditate on yourself in this event for three minutes. You can set a timer or just guess and check a nearby clock.

Then, take a few deep breaths again and clear your mind. Now, select something you think you did not do so well, and see-hear-feel it for one minute *only*.

Immediately after that, take a few deep breaths, and then bring up again the picture and sound and feeling of that first event you did well, and hold your memory of it for another three minutes.

Do this little meditation each night before you go to sleep. It takes only seven minutes a day and begins to work wonders immediately.

Now I'm assuming that you really want to like yourself. No, not just like how you look or the way you dress. I mean really like yourself, who you deeply are. But how can you like yourself if you don't know what that means?

Nobody can give you the answer to that, not even the best paid shrink. Everyone else can only say what it means to like themselves in their own terms.

So you need to discover that on your own. How? Not liking yourself has both a mental belief structure and a physical reality. That usually means your mental attitude drives energies down and your body isn't very healthy. So let's first explore your beliefs on self-like.

THE LIKE-ME SELF-EVALUATION

Here's a simple set of questions you can ask yourself that will help you discover what "liking yourself" really means to you. Let me share this with you. Let's call it the Like-Me Self-Evaluation.

I'll guide you through the questions first, giving some pointers about possible responses. After you have finished, read your responses several times. You will find that some of your answers will lead you to make some adjustments in your thinking and behavior. Things that are important to you will come out, as they may never have before this. It is all part of the process of growing to like yourself better.

When you have time, take a pencil and paper and write down both the questions and the answers on a separate sheet of paper.

Start by stating the outcome you want to achieve.

I want to like myself.

If you think that you already like yourself to some degree, use this statement instead:

I want to like myself more.

Now write down answers the following questions. Be specific with your answers. You want things that will clearly demonstrate to you that you like yourself – as if you were outside you observing yourself. It's okay to have an answer such as "I'd feel better." But that shouldn't be all.

How would I know if I liked myself?

How soon do I want to like myself?

Is it important to me to like myself in any specific situations or with any special people, or all the time?

The first question reflects how impatient you are and how willing you are to give yourself time to grow into liking yourself. The second and third question indicates whether the motivation to like yourself is linked to any certain people or situations. This may give you a clue as to where you can start to put some change into practice.

The next question is in three parts but answer them one at a time. They each will give you a different perspective.

a. **What does not liking myself do for me?**

Absurd as that question may sound, it's based on a sound point. We usually have continued being the way we are because we get some benefit from it, however minimal it might be. If there were nothing, truly nothing, that being this way did for us, then most likely we would have changed already. Looking for the benefit in your present state might not be easy but take some time and think about it.

b. **If I let go of not liking myself, would there be anything I'd lose or give up? Would there be any trade-off?**

Dropping any attitude or behavior has implications, and some of them may be hidden benefits. The old axiom is correct: for everything you lose you gain something, just as for everything you gain you lose something.

c. If I start liking myself, what will that do for me?

Don't try to force answers to this one. Let what comes come. The answers to this might serve as motivations to propel you into action. However, if you're not bursting with answers to this one, perhaps you're not quite ready for change yet. That's perfectly okay.

Answers to these final questions may give you clues as to why you might not be ready and what you can do to achieve a change.

a. What has stopped me from liking myself so far?

You may not be able to answer this question (yet). If you can't, don't worry. Many people find it a challenge. If you can, there are some clues you can use to help you become ready for change.

b. What resources, skills and abilities do I have to help me accomplish this goal?

Here's an opportunity to toot your horn regarding your strengths and qualities!

c. What resources, skills and abilities would I like to have to help me accomplish this?

You can be lengthy or brief, as you like.

d. What's the first step?

Take a good guess at this. Don't settle easily for an automatic "I don't know" response. You know far more about yourself than you think you do.

The goal of this whole process is to give you information on yourself you might not get by any other means. It is simply an organized form of self-talk. If you came up with anything solid on the last question, it may give you the start of an action plan. If not, look at the answers to other questions to give you clues as to how to get into action.

Here are some ideas.

If you find certain resources you would like to have, you can do the process over again using that as your first statement, followed by the questions in the order given. When you get to the last question, you may indeed have a first step that you can begin to put into action.

Here's another approach. Look at your answer that asks you to say what has stopped you from liking yourself so far. If it's a negative, such as "I'm too hard on myself," you will want to state it in the positive to begin this whole process again.

Why? Because the process works to help us achieve goals. We have to state what we want in the positive.

So how can we convert the negative statement we made into a positive? It doesn't work to say, "I want to not be hard on myself." Could you imagine what that would look like – being "not something?" Of course not.

So, to convert the negative to a positive, ask yourself, "If I'm hard on myself, how would I like to be instead?" Maybe you'll say something like "supportive of myself."

So, simply make your opening statement in this manner: "I want to be supportive of myself." Then ask the first question, "How would I know if I did?"

The true value of the meditation we described here, and this self-evaluation process is that they require you to look inward for your answers, not look to others.

As women, when you meditate and become centered you can access an abundance of wisdom and truth.

No one has wiser answers for you than you. They may come from the "you" you already know, or from the "Big You" you are getting to know.

10

AS THEY LAY DYING

*How many millions have recited
the Lord's Prayer their entire life
and missed this most basic point:
"Thy will be done, on Earth
as it is in Heaven?"*

Thy Will, not my will.

As They Lay Dying

I have watched many women dying, and helping others who were dying. I have watched and worked with them through the process. It is a process in which the soul's accumulated worth is tested.

If there is anything that those who face death have in common, it is this single test: to accept the fact that it must not be *my will* but *Thy Will* that prevails.

Few have passed it with flying colors. Most live in *my will*, while God – which is *Thy Will* – is pushed farther and farther away.

Relying on *my will* they fought a hard battle all their life long, and then in the end they fought with *my will* alone and were overcome by the force of death. The ego pushed the body and mind to near-miraculous heights, but, in the end, *my will* died and *Thy Will* prevailed.

To truly live life to the fullest, to reign supreme over all states and attitudes of life, *Thy Will* must prevail while we are still living. That force is unlimited, eternal, and all-powerful. *My will* will only get us into pain and probably sooner dead.

My will creates tears and arguments, eats foul food and smells foul for days afterward, seeks out and reeks of sugar when it feels upset, and leans on lovers when it has no love to give.

I can't count the number of times I've been to a funeral to hear someone eulogized lovingly with the praise, "She lived life the way she wanted it." I wince each time.

How many millions have recited the Lord's Prayer their entire life and missed this most basic point: "Thy will be done, on Earth as it is in heaven?" *Thy Will*, not *my will*.

We know that resistance produces sickness. The unfulfilled needs and wants of the child – from an accumulation of lifetimes' needs and wants gone begging – produces an adult trying to work its way through situations where it can get what it wants. And *my will* is never, ever satisfied.

Daddy wasn't there for us when we needed him. No amount of lovers will ever make up for the loss.

Mom was too much there when we wanted our own space, and no amount of running away will ever give you space enough.

Acceptance is the key. Forgiveness is one of the avenues you can take, but the ultimate path is one of acceptance for all, without judgment of good or bad, right or wrong. Acceptance that the plan was the plan, is the plan and will always be the plan and we are part of that plan, just as we are part of the Infinite Planner and the planning.

That is to say, we are part of God the Creator, part of the ongoing, continuous acts of creating day to day, and we are God who is also the creation itself. The Creator and Creation are one. What is the difference? Energy must pass into form and form must return to energy. It is all a great flow.

Accept that, and know it is happening every day, and you are never apart from Creator. You are the lover of the Beloved and the beloved of the Lover. How, then, can *my will* be apart from *Thy Will*? Strive as hard as anyone can, we are all a part of that Great Will.

Why, then, should women strive so against death?

They are the vessel through which the soul is delivered into life. They cling to that great act of service to Creator. They do not realize they are also the vessels through which the soul can be delivered to eternal life.

With the prayer of a woman, a soul can be released to eternal rest.

At our Womanheart retreat, I had taught the women the chant to help the soul rise after it had passed – a long "Akaal" – which means undying.

She had remembered it and, through her tears over the phone, was asking me to explain again how to use it. Her son had just died in a military training accident, his plane plummeting to Earth, his grave a fiery inferno. There were not even remains of a body left.

 I described the process of chanting Akaal for 11 minutes for 17 days to help the soul break the chains of this life and this planet and rise through the various ethers to the final blue ether that is Creator/Source/Home.

"I can do it, I know I can," I heard her say through her tears.

Her soul had been preparing for this moment a long time. It would be a great sacrifice of self, of her desires to cry for her only child and hold him in her thoughts and thus hold his soul here. Would she have the strength to do it, to send him on?

I did not hear from her for several weeks and then she called and asked to see me.

When she entered my office, the changes she had undergone were immediately obvious. Her face was almost alabaster white and her presence shone like that of an imperial queen. There was an air of absolute calm about her.

"Well I did it. I chanted for 17 days. But before the end I knew I didn't have to go all the way, he was gone. I finished it anyway, just to be sure."

"What happened?" I asked.

"It was about the ninth or tenth day of the chanting. I was doing it in the very early morning, about 5 a.m. While I was chanting he came to me. He was dressed in his best uniform with all his medals and insignias and he had a serene look on his face. He came from behind me and moved up to the front. Then he turned and smiled. He told me a few things, I don't actually remember the words now, but I remember feeling very calm. I knew he was happy. And then he started to move away, stopped and turned and waved to me with an even bigger smile, and then he just moved up and away, faster and faster until I couldn't see him anymore."

"Did you continue chanting?"

"Oh yes, I never stopped, not until several minutes after he left." She wiped a tear from her eye. "He's gone, isn't he?"

"Yes. You sent him home."

"Are you sure?"

"Aren't you?"

"Yes." She put her head on my shoulder and wept silently, tears of relief, not grief.

"Afterwards, I told my daughter-in-law that I knew he was at peace and okay. I didn't tell her how I knew, because I didn't think she could accept what had happened, it is so foreign to the beliefs she was raised with."

"Did she believe you?"

"I don't know. But she seemed more relaxed after that, more relieved."

"You have done a magnificent act," I told her. *"It takes true selfless service to deliver your own child to his final rest. And because of your sacrifice, your service, he does not need to come back again. You have your own special saint in heaven."*

She looked at me incredulously, *"How do you know?"*

I smiled. Had my own experience been so long ago? It seemed like only a couple of years, even though it had been nearly 12 years. *"I delivered my own father by the same means,"* I answered.

"Tell me about it, please."

I was quite different then from the me you know now. I was an executive at a big Park Avenue corporation. My hours were grueling. Only a few years before I had taken vows as a Sikh and put this white turban on my head and had faced ridicule, fear and rage from my compatriots. Someday, perhaps, I'll tell that story. But suffice it to say there had been hard times in which I had truly learned the power of prayer.

My father had been seriously ill several times after my mother had died, including three forms of cancer. In the process of removing the tumors, they had discovered that he had a ballooning area on the aorta just below the heart.

Surgeons tried to remove it and almost lost him on the table. So they sewed him back up and told him some day it would just go 'boom!' and he would be dead, not even knowing what had hit him. He had laughed, saying that was the way he'd always prayed to go anyway, so God had made a beautiful plan for him.

For several years after that, we had wonderful times together. He would occasionally visit me when I lived in the ashram in Brooklyn – rising with me in the pre-dawn hours and watching as we did our yoga and meditations while he sat in a rocking chair in the corner reading his Bible. He spoke with amazement of how healthy and happy I had become.

His only negative comment, delivered more as a joke, was "What's wrong with the King's English?" referring to the old Sanskrit language in which we chanted our meditations. But it didn't really bother him, it was just different. He knew God spoke in all languages.

I would spend weekends whenever I could at his farm, helping him harvest asparagus and corn in the garden, and put up applesauce for the winter. I don't recall ever being happier.

Even when I would fly off for a weekend to some distant city for a yoga gathering with our teacher, Yogi Bhajan, I would always call him from the airport and give him the phone number where he could reach me if he needed me. Each time he took down my spiritual name – since that was how they would know me where I was staying – pronounced it a couple of times to be sure he had it right, and then tell me, 'Have a great time, gal!' He always called me gal, just as he had Mom.

Life was so sweet those years. The father I had never known as a child was finally with me, and we became fast friends. We never spoke of death, rarely even thought if it. Once in a while he would joke about the 'ticking bomb' inside him. But it just became part of Ben's cornball but beloved humor that everyone who knew him loved. He could make people laugh when they felt downright low. It was a gift.

One weekend when I was leaving for yet another city, I asked his help on something financial. Our little ashram family wanted to purchase the house we lived in and approached me about being a substantial buyer. I had a good job but not a lot of assets, so I asked Dad if he would let me borrow against the farm. He had put it in both our names some time before. He thought about it for several minutes. I could hear his inner battle and then, with a sigh, he said, "I can't, gal. It's all I have. You know it's not about you. It's just me. But I want to be there for you in any way I can. I hope you know that." His voice trailed off."

I realized I was crying, and then I heard myself saying it was all right, that I knew he had always been there for me, and not to worry. This was of little consequence.

On the plane flight, I realized that I had leaped back through more than 40 years and forgiven him everything – all the times he hadn't been able to be there for me when I wanted him to provide a buffer between Mom and me. Somehow, I had let all of that go, and I cried quiet tears of relief.

Several weeks later, I was planning to go up to the farm for the weekend and I was rushing to finish up work in the office. I came back after lunch and saw a note stuck onto my phone – a memo pad where some secretary had roughly scratched down the words for me to read, "Your father has died. Call your neighbor Pauline for details."

In horror I read and re-read the note. What? Who? How?

My secretary heard me somehow – perhaps I cried out, perhaps they had been told – and she and others came in.

Someone dialed Pauline's number and I listened.

The old time bomb had gone off. Someone had found him that morning on the floor in front of the TV, the remote control still in his hand, and my cats sitting guard beside him all night. He had started to change channels, and God had changed channels on him. The doctor who came had said he hadn't even known what hit him, had probably experienced no pain at all. Just the way he always prayed for it.

I was in a daze hearing all this. The company gave me a limousine and driver and drove me and one of my spiritual sisters up to the farm – four hours away. Neither of us had ever dealt with death closely before this and we weren't entirely sure what to do. But she could read all the prayers in the old language that I could not yet do, and she knew the immediate things to do.

We had read the prayer for the dead over the body being prepared at the funeral home and gone back to the farm to do the full round of prayers together. She let me sleep a couple of hours and awakened me at 3 a.m. We chanted all seven prayers – usually they are done at various times during the day – and then we sat down in the living room and began the 11-minute chanting of 'Akaal'.

Less than a minute after we started I heard his voice. "Hi, gal," was all he said at first. It was clear and unmistakably Dad.

"Hi, Dad," I answered internally, still continuing the chant.

"Will you be all right, gal?" he asked.

"Yes, Dad. I'll be fine. I have my family now. It's time for you to go home."

"But are you sure you'll be okay?"

"Yes. God has given me all I need. Now you must go home. Go find Mom, she's already there."

He questioned one last time and I heard my voice, like a command, say, "Go home, Dad. Go now!"

All at once I felt as if a giant suction cup had been placed over my head and there was a tremendous pull from the very base of my spine up and outwards. His soul went on a great stream of energy from me, up, up, beyond all reach.

We continued the chant until the little timer beeped at the end. I sat there in a near hypnotic state. Gradually, I told my sister what had happened. We sipped some tea, made breakfast together and tried to figure out what it all meant.

"We were unsure what exactly to do next. So she decided I should call Yogi Bhajan and ask. He was teaching that weekend in Anchorage, Alaska. We dialed the ashram there. Someone picked up the phone and I started to introduce myself. But before I could say what had happened I was cut off by his voice on an extension phone.

"So your father has passed," he said.

"Yes, sir. And we wondered what to do next. Hari Kaur says we have to chant Akaal for 11 minutes for 17 days."

"He does not need your help now," his voice interrupted me.

"But don't we have to chant..."

"I saw you a month ago in Boston and I told you to be at peace and you are and now he is."

My mind still wasn't listening. "But don't we have to..."

"Listen to me, my child. Don't you know what you did? Don't you believe what scripture says, that the prayers of a saint can free the souls seven generations before you and seven generations to come after you?"

Yes, I had read it often in our scriptures, but it had never applied to me. A saint? Hardly. The enormity of what he was saying stopped me.

"Can you not accept what has happened, what you have done?"

"You mean, he is..."

His voice softened. "He is already Home, where you sent him."

He told me that when I returned to New York I could make a meal in Dad's honor and serve it to my little Sikh family.

At that prayer service, I sat behind scripture and took the reading. Wherever the pages fall open, that is deemed to be the specific message. The words read: "God has put a wall between you and your pain. God has released you from the account written in the Akashic records."

And the music sung afterwards was "Guru Dev Mata, Guru Dev Pita" – God is your mother, God is your Father, God is your friend.

And now, here I am 12 years later, resting my head on this good woman's shoulder, feeling her tears of relief and joining with my own.

"So should I do the same thing, make a meal in his honor?" she is asking me.

"Yes, read from your scripture and then serve your family the food you have prepared in his name."

"Did you ever feel his presence again?" She asked me.

"Oh yes, and I saw him. He and mother were both at the funeral, standing by the casket. They were smiling, glowing and surrounded by gold light. My sister, who had come there with me and helped me with the prayers, she saw them too, but nobody else did. The others were all crying. They had lost their gentle Ben.

I told them he was in heaven with Mom and not to cry. He wasn't really gone – every time they cracked a cornball joke they'd heard from Ben, he would still be alive. He would live forever in our hearts.

"And what about now," she asked. "Do you ever feel him near?"

"Yes. And sometimes when I pray to God and Guru Ram Das, I include Ben because I know he's listening. He's part of God."

I realize now what a great blessing God has given me to be able to teach women and touch their hearts. Because I have seen greatness blossom. The gifts have been many. It was a great gift to help this woman learn to meditate and grow over several years, to see her in our classes and watch her become more peaceful when she gained a spiritual name, and then, when the time came, to give her the tools to help her release her child and send him home to God.

The legacy must be passed on. Just this last summer, the opportunity came again.

We were sitting in long lines of men and women holding challenging postures and chanting long beautiful chants, high atop a green-decked mountain in Northern New Mexico. Every summer, over a thousand people from around the world gather here for the Summer Solstice yoga retreat led by Yogi Bhajan.

Several women and men from my classes in Phoenix have come here with me and are growing well through all these challenges. It is near the end of the second day and one of them pulls me aside to ask a question.

"Do you think it would be all right for me to write a prayer for my Dad to be read tomorrow morning at services?" she asks.

Her face is lined with worry. She came here against the better judgment of virtually everyone in her family who felt her father's cancer was close to taking him and she should be by his side. The longing of her soul brought her here but her mind was not at rest about it.

"Of course it would be okay. It would be beautiful. Even though he hasn't passed yet, you could ask for blessings on his soul that is choosing to transition at this time. At the very least, it will help him through the pain."

She writes the prayer – a daughter's request for blessing in anticipation of death – and later reads it to me. It is quite touching.

The next morning at dawn, after meditations are finished and the service of song and prayer is held, the lady who stands up to read the prayers picks up a number of them laid in front of the altar. She starts to read and then she gets to the special one we have both been waiting for. It is a few seconds before we realize that she has departed from the exact wording and is paraphrasing it, asking for blessings on the soul of the father who has transitioned! She spoke as if he had already died.

We are shocked. The face of his daughter is confused. Well, it is all right. He received a blessing. He will do with it whatever God wishes.

Hours later, during our lunch break, I hear her name called. She comes over to me, the lines deep in her face. It is a call from home. Will I come with her?

As she listens over the phone, I see the tears come and the pall of grief take the blood from her face. Her father has passed.

She puts the phone down and cries. It had happened only three hours after the prayer had been read that morning. And in that time, virtually everyone important to him had called, not knowing the wisdom of their timing, but sensing they should "check in". Even the priest from his church had called.

Some would have called it all a matter of synchronicity. But it was all part of God's plan – planting the idea in her to write the prayer, having it read as if he had passed, and in that way opening the door for the soul to take its exit homeward.

She asked me what to do and I told her that in the evening, after the day's course was finished, we would read all the prayers for him and then chant Akaal.

Huddled in my tent on my little mattress, we finished the prayers in the wee small hours of the morning. She had fallen asleep on my mattress before the prayers finished but I had continued them until the end. Then, waking her, we chanted Akaal together.

"Has he gone?" she asked afterwards.

"Yes," I replied. She had not felt him there, or seen anything, but somehow knew he had gone. So too did I, though I did not explain it further.

He had gone before we had even begun the prayers. He had gone on that beautiful burst of energy from the prayer she had written which God had read for him the morning before. What we had done was to seal his

*going for her, to complete her great deed of service and
continue a tradition which she in her time would pass
on to others.*

*She would chant Akaal for 11 minutes a day for the
next 17 days.*

*During that time, she was earning the spiritual name
she had just received.*

*It would take a while for her to realize the enormity of
what she had done. That she had been the instrument of
deliverance for her own father. That, in leaving his
bedside to come to this place of meditation and prayer,
she had left her past behind and had chosen a brighter
future than she might have had.*

*And as she came to realize this, over months and years,
she would stand as a symbol of courage for countless
other women. The courage to leave the past, to live in
the present and make a new future.*

This woman had brought souls into this world and helped
release them to eternity. Each woman has this same gift.

THE GIFTS OF DYING

I have watched those who are dying give gifts to the living
months, days, moments before they pass. Sometimes the gift
has to do with a life lesson they needed a long time before.
Sometimes it is a gift that brings whole new life to the
receiver.

One woman who was a nurse of many years and had seen countless people die, called me when her husband was rushed into the hospital in the final throes of Lou Gehrig's disease. His lungs had closed up on him and his throat could barely rattle each gulp of life.

"What do I do for him?" she asked me.

"Chant with me as his soul goes," I said, holding her hand as she leaned over him.

The last breath came – that strange sound matched by nothing else I have ever heard as the final exhale brings the breath evenly and with equal force out of both nostrils for the only time in each person's life.

I started the chant and she joined in. We repeated it together and continued for eleven minutes. Midway through it I heard her gasp, but she quickly rejoined me.

When we finished, she squeezed my hand. She was smiling even though her face was flushed with emotion and tears.

"I saw it," she sputtered out the words. "I saw his soul rise, just like you said. It was beautiful."

I had seen it too but would not have mentioned it had she not first.

"It was like a thin smoke," she said, painting a picture with her hand. "It rose gently from the top of his head and went up through the ceiling."

I told her to chant each day for 17 days to help his soul continue on to its final destination. She did that, though she saw nothing more. It did not matter. When she had *helped him with that first liftoff, she had already received the gift.*

One of the strangest and most beautiful gifts I have ever received from someone who was dying gave me an entirely new and awesome awareness of God's intended mission for me in this lifetime.

It happened in an instant, and it changed both of us forever. Without that exchange between us, he might have died then and I might not have lived to a fuller capacity unknown to me before that.

I will use real names, actual details and facts here, because all the people involved long since this happened have told the events to all, so much so that it has become a piece of legend around these parts.

His name was Charles and his wife was Agnes. I do not remember how and when I met them except that I knew them by their spiritual names – Daya Singh and Daya Kaur (the lion and the princess of God's mercy and compassion). I knew when I met them that I had known them both forever.

They were members of our growing community of yoga students, but unlike many students they were both also attracted to the sacred music of our Sikh path, and so I saw them in my yoga classes and also at our temple services.

Daya Singh, with a dark and peppered beard, looked a bit like a wild old bear, but his heart shone through in his warm brown eyes. Daya Kaur served his needs with absolute attentiveness and love, following him everywhere but leading his voice with her stronger voice whenever the singing started.

We didn't talk very often. There was no need for words, so much seemed already shared between us. A passing hug, a smile was all we needed to show.

And then one day Daya Kaur called me to tell me the sad news. He had been diagnosed with a brain tumor and it was quite large – a side effect, she was told, of the asthma medication he had been taking for over two decades. Surgery was imminent.

"Will you come and pray with me before and after the surgery?" she asked.

"Of course."

She made sure he had a tape recorder playing his special sacred music at his bedside for hours before the surgery. As he left on the gurney for the O.R., I saw his face lit with the rosy glow that came whenever he sang that music.

I had to go back to my office but promised to return when he was out of surgery.

Her call took me by surprise a few hours later. The doctors had almost lost him on the table, she said, and had to stop the surgery, with the tumor still remaining lodged inside. He was convulsing and not expected to live through the night.

"Please come," her voice urged.

I entered the room and immediately was struck with the smell and look of death in the air, a heaviness the normal eye could not see, a sickly sweet smell the normal nose would not detect. What could I do? My mind cried out hopelessly.

I put my hands together in prayer, standing beside his bed, seeing his body lurching with each convulsion, his strained hands and feet so crudely strapped down. I remember my prayer exactly as the words came silently to my mind, "Well God, I guess if you want him he's yours. But if you don't, and you can use me in some way, then please do."

Instantly, a strong male voice spoke commandingly in the back of my head. "Put your hands over his head."

"Yes, sir," I heard myself reply, and I reached out through all the connections linking him to instruments and monitors to put my palms directly over his head. His brain felt like fireworks under my hands, like some crazy Frankenstein monster shorting out.

I closed my eyes and felt the energy flow through me to him, turning me for a moment ice-cold and forcing me to lean against the railing of the bed.

It had not occurred to me to go to his bedside and use a newly-trained skill I had acquired only a few months before when I had taken a weekend class in an Oriental form of healing called Reiki. And it never occurred to me to question what I was doing there at his bed. I was simply following orders.

I had heard that clear strong voice several times in my life and I had always done what it had told me to do. It had never been wrong and I knew it never would be.

I closed my eyes and let the energy pump through me into him, first going to his head and then down into his chest. After about ten minutes, I heard his breathing shift and he began to snore. "Good, he's passing into sleep," I thought happily, my eyes still closed as my hands moved slowly down over his abdomen.

After a total of about fifteen minutes, I felt a total shift under my hands and I opened my eyes. The first thing I saw were his hands relaxed by his side. I looked down and his feet were also relaxed.

Daya Kaur was standing at the foot of the bed, her mouth open in shock and surprise. "I wish I'd had a camera," she said.

"Why?" I asked.

"Look, look at the monitors."

She pointed out the blood pressure. When I had started the energy fifteen minutes before, it had been 187 over 135 and they had been unable to stop its climb with medications. Now, after the energy, it stood at 137 over 85. It never rose again.

The doctors came in, saw the change, and told her that he was not out of the woods yet. They explained that the tumor was pressing against vital areas that would leave him partially paralyzed and most likely unable to speak.

I simply said to her I'd be back in the morning to give him more Reiki.

The next morning when I arrived, Daya Singh was already out of ICU in a standard semi-private room. He had fewer tubes connecting him to instruments, though he was still on IV feeding and he had not yet awakened.

I moved behind his bed and put my hands over his face from behind him.

Within a few minutes, he opened his big brown eyes and looked up at me, whispering quite audibly, "Thank you!"

Great, he's going to talk, I thought happily, smiling back at him.

I worked for an hour over him, came back in the afternoon and did another hour. The next morning he was sitting up, feeding himself and using the bathroom under his own power.

There was even more progress over the next twenty-four hours.

Then, to everyone's surprise except Daya Kaur's and mine, on the morning of the fourth day, he drove himself home from the hospital.

His trials and tribulations weren't over, however. They gave him the wrong asthma medication and he had a bad reaction, putting him back in for a day. Then they started radiation treatments and by the third dose he broke out into epileptic seizures. I came to the hospital every day for nearly two weeks, each time the signs getting better. But I knew his soul was struggling about staying with us. He wanted to go Home, but part of him wanted to stay with us to continue to be the "big bear" protector for his beloved Daya Kaur.

That part won out and the "miracle man" as we all called him by then came out of the hospital again. This time the doctors' prediction was that he wouldn't live long, the tumor still being lodged in place. So I told him

I'd see him for Reiki once a day for forty days – that all-important yogic change cycle. The tumor went away but I continued daily treatments for over 60 days.

They told him it would be back in less than three years. It never did come back.

His life changed forever, as had mine. His gift to me was the understanding that God wanted me to re-examine who and what I thought I was and move into a larger role of service to others than I had thought possible.

He lived lovingly, asthma and all, for another eight plus years until a fall, a broken bone that did not heal right and a resulting infection made life too difficult for him to bear. During those years, I became a strong healer, with the courage to live in God's will, not my will, helping many people and always citing the "big bear" with gratitude for the gift he awoke in me.

Near the end, he told me that he wanted "to go Home", and when I asked him if he meant little home or big Home, he smiled and whispered "big Home". I told him to use the energy I gave him from that day forward to talk to God and see what God wanted for him.

He declined fairly rapidly after that, often barely conscious when I would visit his hospital bed. Then one day when I came in, he sat up, his face bright, eyes clear and voice strong and distinct as it had not been for a long time. He told me that the form of healing I was doing was "the last ring", as he put it.

He was not talking about Reiki because, as he had experienced my work over the years since I first began healing work, he had recognized the change in the energy flowing through me, as did I. I could call on Reiki and did often, but then I called on something else and it came easily.

He spoke clearly to me that morning of the "first ring" that had been Kundalini Yoga and Tantric Yoga, and the second ring that held the forms of healing we use that are on the body or close to it. Then he said this was the last ring and the final healing form we would need. "After this form, we do not need anything else," were his final words.

He slipped back into a semi-trance sleep and from that day forward he never again spoke a rational sentence longer than a two or three-word phrase.

I pondered over his words for some time, knowing I would eventually relay them to Yogi Bhajan for his insights. But I had little time to do that, as my dear friend was slipping fast. And then, one night, when I would have gone to his hospital bed, something delayed me late after a class I taught. A student asked me about his condition and I heard myself reply, "He will pass in a few hours."

That night, oddly, I did not go to the hospital. Neither did his wife or any of his other friends. Something stopped us all. It was his time and he had to cross over on his own.

The next day we all stood at the side of his white-cloth-draped body in the funeral parlor, reciting prayers, and then followed the hearse to the crematorium where the body would be incinerated.

With the initial prayers completed before the body was committed to the flames, all the others left except Daya

Kaur and me. We sat outside the giant ovens and I recited for an hour and a half all the prayers, as I said I would, to help him cross over and go Home. I never looked up once, even though I felt much happening. My eyes remained on the pages with the words I was chanting.

Daya Kaur told me she had seen him standing in an open doorway with intensely pure white light beyond. She saw him turn, she saw Yogi Bhajan there to help as he had promised, and then Daya Singh had looked at us both, smiled and passed effortlessly into the light.

When I finished he was gone, not even a whisper of his presence remaining.

There are few gifts you can give someone at death. All I could give was the gift of the prayers he so loved to help him on his way. Perhaps that was all he needed.

He was a man that showed hundreds of people that miracles still happened, even to so-called little people. So all of us could have hope and some of us a certain knowledge that God lives in us every day.

Thank you, dear friend. You gave us all so very much.

11

JUDGE NOT!

*Judgement is the coffin in which
kindness, the heart, is buried.*

*Judge someone, anyone,
and you might as well bury them.*

Judge Not!

What do you think is the greatest cause of marriage breakup? Another woman, leading to infidelity? No. One partner travels a lot on business? No. Many marriages have survived while partners have been separated for weeks, even months. I had one client who saw her husband only one weekend every two months for three years until economic circumstances changed and they could be together.

The cause of breakup will surprise you, because the absence of it also underlies the strength of a true union.

The single most important cause of breakup is judgement- one partner criticizes and then judges the other.

It does not matter whether the judgement is based on fact - whether one partner actually did or said something wrong - or whether it is a creation of fear or anger-driven fantasy and the accused is innocent of the charge. Judgement itself is the killer. Accumulated over time it can deal the death blow to any partnership.

When love begins to die, it falls to judgement. The end of the line is often a brief comment. For the man it may be simply, "She isn't the same woman I married," and of course he did not want her to change. For the woman it is, "He changed," meaning not in the way that she wanted him to change.

Judgement is the coffin in which kindness, the heart, is buried. Judge someone, anyone, and you might as well bury them.

In poor child-rearing language, it means taking something the kid did wrong, - "That was a bad thing you did!" - and turning it into, "You're a bad boy."

Do that often enough and you might as well put the other person in a coffin. You will never be able to reach through the wall you have created to get at the real individual. For the relationship to have a chance, the man may occasionally fall into judgement, but the woman must never judge. Her criticism of him will dry up the juice of kindness. Without the woman's heart, the marriage is over.

Think of how quickly it happens. There are many starting points. Here's one.

He does something that seems clearly thoughtless to her. She mentions it. He barks back at her defensively. She criticizes him. It snowballs. She becomes sensitive to similar things in him. He becomes aggressively charged around her and begins to criticize first the little things about her, then bigger and bigger.

After awhile it becomes a subconscious, even conscious, battle to see who can criticize first. They become reluctant to speak around each other for fear of giving out more ammunition. They are destroying each other, eating up the "nicer selves" they married.

Once judgement starts to snowball, they throw away tons of good times they had together in order to sort through and find only the bad times. They keep rehashing and remembering only those. Judgement soon becomes blind.

Have you not read the command, "Judge not lest you be judged?"

For all too many couples, marriage vows appear to have given them the right to judge, imprison and punish each other endlessly, even to pass that process on to their kids who will, in time, pass it on to their partners and their children.

Know this to be true:

> *There is nothing and no one bad or wrong until it is labeled and judged so.*

If you call someone bad or wrong, not only do you cut yourself off from being a positive influence in their lives but also you miss participating in the very real fun process of their growth from that point forward.

Do it a number of times and you have turned your back on the other person. You lose.

And what happens to the person who does the judging? Does it stop there, with his partner? No, it proceeds to others. His children, friends, people on the job, most certainly his parents – where it all started anyway, even while he was in the womb!

Those who judge take it upon themselves to judge all others. They become enraged and soon they become outraged, blasting out at strangers, at people who jaywalk, at people who park their cars in handicapped places without the proper license plates. They become the judges of all wrongdoing, or what appears to be wrongdoing in their eyes.

And that is their undoing. They call down upon themselves the rage of others – so many people share this rage script nowadays. Remember the invective: As you judge so shall you be judged,

The only person you have the birthright-permission to judge is yourself and then only at the point of death as the soul leaves the body. At that point, for a few seconds, you see the film of your whole life and you judge yourself through that. Before death, your vision is limited. At death, the consciousness becomes vast and you can judge the whole panorama of your life with the eyes of the Infinite.

Consider this alternative: if you do not judge someone, forgiveness is not necessary. It is meaningless. You only need to forgive someone who has wronged you, that is to say someone you judged as having wronged you. Yet if you continue to judge and show it, no amount of forgiveness will be believed and accepted.

HOW IT ALL BEGINS

How does this cycle of criticizing and judging start? Obviously, long before the partnership begins. It takes a mindset programmed early in life with observations of parents and other adults.

There are three ways this behavior can ignite.

First, the universal and hardest to change attitude is that which in anger seeks a scapegoat, usually choosing the nearest and dearest.

Second, the woman shows herself to have some flaw, which may be a pet peeve of his. At some point he seeks to correct her. His fragile limits of trust went beyond bearable limits. An extension of this is her negative self-talk, or revealing of negative self-history, a habit of many women that draws down men's criticism on them.

Thirdly, she criticizes him, or holds him up to ridicule, often innocently at first, and worst of all in public. He strikes back in rage.

Let's look at each one from the dynamics of the two genders.

Scapegoating is more often than not a male defensive ploy from early childhood when, accused by Mom or fearing accusation, he points the finger to the nearest person as the real culprit. That's not to say that women don't scapegoat. They do occasionally, especially given some family histories.

Girls are regularly set up to find fault in themselves while young men are trained not to be introspective but to get into action. So whatever needs correcting, in their eyes, is generally outside them and needs to be fixed.

That is why, when women tell their husbands or boyfriends their negative thoughts and histories, men try to fix them.

This is the most difficult behavior for women to accept in a man. Even if she does nothing to provoke it, she cannot easily see a set-up coming or gracefully find a way out. The accuser's ongoing assumption is "somebody did something wrong" and, by implication, it is not them.

I still remember the frustrations of learning to operate my first personal portable computer in 1980. When I finally got into the word processing program, its response to one of my tries was to lock up and display the friendly message: "One of us must have made an error." I knew exactly which one the finger was pointing at.

"It all started with his habit of losing things. That's what started our breakup."

The woman sitting across from me is recounting the failure of her third marriage. At age 36, she is close to judging herself marriage-unworthy.

"He would leave his hair shampoo somewhere, or misplace the keys to his car and each time accuse me of taking them or putting them somewhere. It got so he accused me of having this little conspiracy against him."

"How did you handle it?" I asked, knowing she most likely had no clue and only the parental models of failure to draw upon.

"I tried to tell him I didn't take anything. I hadn't even seen those things."

"In other words, you argued with him."

"I didn't intend to."

"But that's the way he saw it. You were arguing with him."

"Yes, I guess so." She wiped a tear from her cheek. "I don't know what else I could have done."

I sighed inwardly. "Well there isn't much. You have to lighten things up, help him look for the lost item, then make light of the matter when you find it."

"How will that help?"

"He'll see you genuinely looking for it, not just automatically going to where you knew it was all along. That gives him a subtle hint he was wrong in his assumption. Also, when he makes that accusation, he does it because he feels helpless, alone. If you help him, he may just back off some of that helpless stuff."

"But what if he was right and I did move it?"

"So what? This isn't about deciding who's right or wrong. It's about taking responsibility for fixing the problem. Don't confuse the issue. The issue is where is the missing item, right?" She nods her head. "If you make yourself the problem, then it's a much bigger issue. He has to fix you. And if you let him make you angry, you react to being labeled, and then in your eyes

the problem also becomes him. So you go from 'he has a problem' to believing 'he is the problem' – right? You have to break the cycle that escalates a small behavioral problem into a big people problem. If that repeats often enough, it becomes a major issue between you."

Scapegoating tends to jump into big-size issues fast, with words like "you always do that," or "you never do this." So I warned her she had to act fast. The secret was to go for the solution to the immediate situation, to immerse herself in being helpful, and not let it escalate.

Although she was already separated from her husband, and therefore couldn't try out a new approach on him, she was able to alter her behavior with her eight-year-old son who had picked up the behavior of his father, her second husband. It was interesting that all three men she had married had the same judgmental approach. Most likely, so also did her father.

Now let's look at the second way criticism can ignite – her revealing of her negative history.

In some ways it can be related to scapegoating. The man is predisposed to look for what he perceives to be flaws or problems in others – despite how much good-working stuff may be in evidence.

Couples like this remind me of a mated pair of birds. They both look pretty sitting on their perch, but they take turns picking on each other, finding some small feather not quite in place or messing around until there are several big ones to be straightened out. In bird language it's called preening, but in human terms and to someone who is the preener's preenee, it can feel like being picked on.

When a man doesn't have something to do, something that needs fixing, he looks for something, anything he can find. If his mate is picking on herself or on him, he may start picking on his mate. The solution is to not ignite the process. See that he needs something to do, suggest something practical that may even be fun. Then compliment him on it while he's doing it, admire it when he's done, and he'll be happy.

This approach really isn't as manipulative as it may sound. It's just good sense. If you don't do that, you will have to spend a lot of time sitting in front of the TV, living vicariously through melodramas. Then you're not living your own lives. You're living someone else's lives that aren't even real.

Often they're a reenactment and re-enforcement of the very negative behavior you would like to see changed. On the manipulation scale, that type of behavior – the TV-for-hours pacifying remedy – is far more manipulative and destructive.

What underlying desire creates a judgmental person? A desire to control circumstances and people. It is fear-driven and connected directly into the self-survival mechanisms.

His desire to preen you is driven by his fear there might be something amiss about you, something that would go awry and threaten his focus elsewhere and thus his entire sense of balance. He has very little time for big problems, other than at his job. He picks on the little ones he sees in you, in the hope that that is all there are.

How do you deal with this? First off, don't let it bother you. If you don't attach to an occasional straightening of your hair, or dusting off your shoulder, he won't attach much to it either.

If the preening goes too far for your tastes, distract him with something else more positive. He'll forget his other momentary itch.

TELLING IT ALL

The deeper cause of judgmental behavior comes from the woman herself – her own deprecating self-talk and the revealing of her less than inspiring history.

If women have a partnership death-wish it is revealed in this one behavior – they must "air their dirty laundry" to their lover. In all the clients I see, this is the most frequent cause for breakup and the one they seem to be totally unable to see in themselves.

The young woman is in her late forties and she has just described herself in the negative for the fifth time in less than five minutes in my office.

"I screw up all the time," she started off with.

After several other negative comments, she repeated this one again. I stopped her right there. "How many times a day do you say that?" I asked.

"Say what?" She was totally unaware of her own language.

"You just said, 'I screw up all the time.' You said it twice in the past five minutes."

She winced when I said the words. "Well it's true!"

"So you believe. Do you say it out loud a lot, or mostly just think it?"

"I don't know. I guess I mostly think it."

"So you've convinced yourself and, to prove it, you make a lot of mistakes, right? And then people believe you when you say it out loud because you've piled up a lot of evidence."

She looked hurt. "I don't understand. What has this got to do with my marriage?"

I smiled, touching her hand gently. "I was just demonstrating to you one reason why your partner is critical of you. He is picking up on your own self-criticism."

"Well everybody else picks on me. Maybe they're all right."

I shifted approach, since she was stuck in a rut. "Has there been a time when you really screwed up and you did something okay, maybe even well?"

She looked at me in surprise. "Well I made a couple of great babies. Even Frank says I make good babies."

"Great. So you don't screw up all the time. And I bet they're great kids still. How old are they?"

She smiled. "We had neat times those early days, when Ginny and Peter were little. But then they grew up and now they're teenagers and having big problems in school. I guess the old screw-up me came back after a short vacation."

"Who told you so?"

"Frank."

"Before or after you blamed yourself out loud for their problems?"

She paused a moment then said very softly, "After I said it to me and then to him."

"So now you know what to do, right?"

"No, what?"

"First, stop repeating your internal putdowns out loud, to him or anyone else. Then stop thinking them."

I watched the thought dawn on her face, and then the puzzling process take over. "How?"

"Put a muzzle over your mouth, connected directly to an editor in your brain. Stop before you speak anything, take an extra couple of breaths while you re-speak in your mind what you were going to say. If it has any negative in it, direct or indirect, throw it in the mental garbage can. Think how easily you can do that. Try it now."

Her face went through its downcast look and then brightened. "Yes, I can do that. Of course I can't guarantee all the time."

"Just start. It'll catch on. After awhile the muzzle and the editor will be built in, acting quickly and automatically to filter out the negative stuff."

I reviewed my notes on her partnering history and saw how well she had told stories of past situations casting her in a negative light.

"You probably told Frank about the extra-marital affair you had while you were still married to your second husband, right?"

Her cheeks reddened. "Yes. I thought he should know."

"He is not your father-confessor. He is not God. What did you expect him to think when you told him that garbage?"

"I don't know. I guess I didn't think he would think it applied to us."

"Right, you didn't think. Look, I don't mean to be hard on you, I just want you to wake up and realize what evidence you've given this man to distrust you and now you wonder why he is so critical of you. He's afraid of you. He's afraid he can't rely on you, that you'll get involved with someone on the sly, that you'll screw up in some way important to him and his survival as a relatively sane, happy man. Men aren't as complex as women. They can't hold as many problems and potential problems as we can, processing and reprocessing them as we do. They're action oriented. They try to take some action to fix them. And the fixes look like Band-Aids and sometimes there are a few too many and they walk away."

"What can I do?"

"First of all, stop accusing yourself. Drop your own judgments, forgive yourself and accept the fact that you've always done the best you could at the time, all your life. If afterwards you review it and judge yourself, that's not fair. Have you ever consciously tried to do something badly?"

She laughed. "Of course not."

"So how dare you tell yourself you're not good enough. Get the voices of your mother or father out of your head. Establish your own voice. Congratulate yourself at the time you do something for doing the best job you

could. Build up some good credits with yourself. Occasionally, you can even repeat them to Frank, and to others."

I had her make a list on paper of some things she did well over the past 24 hours, and then helped her make a pact with herself to write down three or four each day until the next time I saw her.

Did it work? Well, it started a process. Will it save the marriage? It's too soon to tell, because marriages rise or fall due to various factors. But this one appears to be working better now.

For many women, when they meet a new man, there seems to be some primordial drive to "tell all" – all the bad things in their life, including recent events during the early stages of their courtship. It is almost like a death wish.

There is nothing more dampening of ardor in a relationship than bad news about what seems to him to be a good woman. Maybe that is why good women are so hard to find.

I could hear his exasperation over the phone. "Why did she have to tell me that crap?" he asked. His newly-discovered lady love, living on the other coast, had just told him she'd goofed and had a one-night stand at a party two days after he left her. "I told her I'd be back in a month, and that we're just right for each other. Didn't she believe me? And even if she wasn't sure, why did she have to tell me about that guy?"

I told him I didn't know, but I would call Judy and talk with her. It was a fib on my part. I was all too sure I understood what had happened. Of course, it wasn't the first thing she would divulge.

"I just had too much to drink," she confessed the moment she got on the phone. "And I wanted to be perfectly honest with Jim. I wanted him to know I had done this terrible thing, so there wouldn't be anything between us. I believe in truth."

I almost laughed at her wording. "Judy, you're not in a court of law. This is not the guy you swear to and say, 'the whole truth and nothing but the truth'. He isn't your judge and he isn't the person you need to look to for a pardon. That person is you and God within you. That's who you need to tell the whole truth to."

"But I was so afraid that what happened with my husband would happen all over again, you know. He found out I had an affair and then he left me."

"How did he find out?"

She halted a moment and then blurted it out. "I told him."

"You told him?"

"Yes. He would have found out anyway."

"Not unless you mumbled the wrong name when you were in bed together. Husbands don't come with god-like psychic powers. You are just afraid of screwing up and being found out, just like when you were a kid, right? So you tell Daddy first and he pats you on the back or hugs you and says, 'It's okay and I love you anyway'. Right?"

"Something like that."

"But your husband didn't do that, did he?"

"Well he did at first, or at least I thought so. He was so thoughtful. We were the best of friends, really, for six months after I told him about it. And then, all at once with no warning, he said he couldn't take it anymore and he left me. Just like that."

"That shows you how long he was trying to swallow what you told him. So now you're going to try Jim out to see if he's like Daddy. Or was Daddy really like that?"

"He was. He really loved me for what I am."

"At least for what you were as a child. These men want to see you as trustworthy, as a Goddess, and you blow holes in their dream. There aren't many men who can live with that, even if they have a masochistic streak."

"So should I lie to him?"

I smiled at the simplicity of it. "No, I didn't say to tell an untruth. Did Jim ask you if you loved being with him when he was there?"

"Yes."

"And what did you answer?"

"Well yes, of course."

"Good, that was the truth. And when he asked you if you were happy to get his phone calls, you told him yes. And were you looking forward to seeing him again, and you said yes."

"Yes, yes..." I could hear her crying now. "But I didn't tell him the whole truth about that night with that man. Oh I just hate to tell you, you'll think I'm not worth talking to."

"That's not likely. Go on."

"Well, do you know the drug Ecstasy?" I hummed yes. "I was taking some and I guess I lost control and before I knew it we were in bed together and I couldn't stop things even though I wanted to."

I sighed audibly.

"Am I that awful?" she asked in a very little girl voice.

"No, I was thinking how you were asking forgiveness for the wrong thing. Not just asking the wrong person, but about the wrong thing. Do you know what you did wrong that evening?"

"What?"

"You turned yourself over to a drug, the man was incidental. You opted out of choice and decision making. You went AWOL from the present into a half-world fantasy. What did that do for you?"

"Nothing. At least nothing good."

"Well it must have seemed like it would do something for some part of you or you wouldn't have done it."

"So should I tell Jim?"

"Of course not. That would only confuse him more and do nothing for you. You can clean up this situation, can't you? You don't need someone else to smooth it over for you, do you? Talk it out to yourself in your prayer time in the morning. You know, that quiet time you take before sunrise when you talk to God. Do your meditations, raise your spirit, and then talk to God. That's the only place where you can take your problems

and get real answers without paying a big price. God will never let you down, you know that."

"That's when I can be really truthful?"

"That's when you can learn how to live your truth. Telling truths or lies isn't the real issue. It's living your truth, the truth of who you are and who you are becoming. If you went out to parties like that often, then you'd be on the way to becoming a different person than the lady I know who gets up and does her meditations and prayers every morning. Just keep doing those mornings and that's the person you'll grow into, more and more. That's the person Jim loves, the person you want to love."

"So I'm in conflict with myself?"

"A little. But you're working to resolve the conflict. He can't work that out for you. He'll try to fix it, make it go away, because he doesn't understand it. Don't burden him with your work. You see, the mind can get overwhelmed, confused sometimes, but the strength of the spirit and the soul in you are obvious. Do you not feel the strength inside waking you in the morning?"

"Yes. But I'm afraid."

"Afraid of what?"

"If I go so far that way, if I get too spiritual, maybe I won't stay grounded, I won't be someone Jim can love because I won't need a man, not in the way he wants me to need him. And it's really important to me to love him. He is so very special."

"You turn those worries over to God. A truly spiritual woman isn't needy. She will draw to herself a spiritual

man, who also isn't needy, and there is plenty of passion and earthiness in that joining."

"So I don't have to tell Jim everything?"

It was like listening to a last gasp of the old logic. "No. Tell him about who you really are and are becoming even more, a beautiful flower, a jewel, a truly gifted spiritual woman. Are you not that person?"

"I guess..."

"Say 'Yes!' like you believe it."

"Yes...yes!"

"Good. Now go talk to God and build that jewel more and more each day."

The simple fact is something we've known a long time: you are who you believe you are. More specifically, *you are who you say you are. You are who you live and demonstrate yourself to be.*

Judy had started a meditative process because she wanted to believe herself to be a better person, a jewel as I put it. All she has to do is to continue accumulating evidence in that direction. Her work so far had drawn to her a special man who saw her as a special lady.

To believe a momentary glitch would be to invite falling back on old beliefs about herself. You cannot totally do away with so-called bad behavior, but you can replace it and overwhelm it with what we will call good behavior. This is how anyone can re-form themselves.

In some ways it's a lot like stopping smoking. You don't really give up cigarettes. It doesn't work. Instead, take up some good activity, something healthy like yoga and yogic breathing, and gradually it will replace the old neediness that supported the old habits.

In other words, make a habit out of being a better you.

PUBLIC RIDICULE AND JEALOUSY

Now let's look at the third route by which judgment grows and overcomes relationships – holding your partner up to public ridicule. This is done equally by both men and women, though men find it unforgivable.

Women do this mostly due to jealousy. First it grows silently, walking on little cat feet, unnoticed by the man, even unnoticed by the woman. Then she realizes it, tries to fight it with logic – that rarely works longer than the first or second time of suspicion. Then, fueled by her own insecurity, it spills out of her mouth at him, often in the presence of others.

Men cannot cope with accusation and distrust. If there is one thing that will cause them to cut off almost instantly from the woman, it is this act of public shame. It assaults their identity, and to a man this is who he is.

To a woman, public identity is only an outer frame of who she is. Though being held up to public ridicule is demoralizing to her, in many instances she is already shaming and degrading herself with her own inner talk. But to the man, with his identity assaulted, he may well throw away his accuser and go on to re-establish his identity in new eyes.

I cannot believe what this beautiful, still-young-in-appearance woman, mother of two children and wife to their father for 17 years is telling me. It is a horrible story of marriage breakdown. Of all people to feel jealousy toward other women, she would seem to be far from the top of the list.

"I just couldn't help myself," she was saying through her tears. "Women would gather around him at parties and he would dance with them. He was actually laughing and enjoying it, enjoying being with them."

"So you spoke out in front of them all?" I asked incredulously.

"I just couldn't help it. I think I even shouted."

"And this happened last year?"

"Yes. He has barely been civil with me ever since. And now he's asked for a divorce."

"Do you want a divorce?"

"No, of course not. I want him to love me. He used to love me, in the beginning."

"But you don't trust him, or do you now?"

"Well..." she looked away, avoiding my eyes.

"Can you trust him?" I pursued.

"No." She turned back to look at me, her eyes glazed with tears. "He never looks at me anymore with a smile. But he looks at every other woman and smiles and laughs with them. What can I do to get him back?"

I feel myself taking a deep inhale before I speak. Should I tell her it may be too late to do anything? That once a man is ridiculed, it doesn't take long before he turns off and turns his back, and when that happens he hardly ever reconsiders. "It may be too late. How hard are you willing to work?"

"I'll do anything."

"Anything?" She nods her head. "Then suggest he go to some party and have a good time. Go to several parties. Don't you go with him. And don't ask him about it afterwards. And if he says anything about it you just say, 'Great! I'm happy you had fun.' In other words, start looking and sounding like you trust him."

"Okay, but I'll probably go nuts thinking about what he's doing!"

"Fine. But go nuts away from him where he can't see it. Don't you understand? He looks at the pain in your face and it's like an accusation to him. At some point he might follow some other woman's temptation just on the whim that if you believe he's playing around he might as well go enjoy himself."

"Do you think he's playing around now?"

"I have no idea, but that's not the point, is it? The point is you want him to respond happily to you again, right? You want him to show love and kindness to you, right? So you have to show him your happy, trusting face. Who knows, if you smile enough around him you may actually change your own feelings."

"Will he believe me?"

"At first, no. But if you remain consistent, he will be confused, then curious, and then he'll test the waters with you."

"What do you mean?"

"He'll invite you to a party and do what he usually does and watch for your negative reaction."

"Oh God, I don't know if I can hide my feelings."

"Sure you can. I'll give you a little mental trick you can do to help yourself. Just picture everyone wearing Mickey Mouse ears and then put them on a film and run it backwards and forwards several times. It will take the seriousness out of it and give you an edge."

"How long will it take before he believes me?"

"A few times. Maybe four or five. Stay occupied with other people. Act as if he isn't even there. You can do it."

"I'll try."

"No, don't try. Just do it."

When she left my office, I sent her off with a silent prayer on my lips. I knew she was going up against impossible odds. Because the challenges she faced were not outside, but inside herself. The self can be a terrible prison.

Most women are not even aware they are locked in a prison. When they realize it, they see no safety anywhere else, because those tight walls are the whole world they know. They see other women who seem to have freedom, who act more joyfully and have choice. But they might as well be on an alien planet - getting to that place seems so impossibly distant to them.

OUT OF THE PRISON OF SELF

If I could have given this client an injection of some miracle balm, it would have been a month of Womanheart retreats. A month of days spent rising early in the morning to do yoga and meditation, to grow strong with other women experiencing their growing strength. A month of nights filled with the bliss of healing energies shared among themselves.

There was simply no way that giving her mind games and bolstering up her confidence for an hour could prepare her for the task she faced.

To win the battle of self she was facing, she had to do more than take back her power from this man. She had to build power within herself, a power she had never had before, a true power that enlightened women possess. A power that says: "I need no one. I need no thing. I am who I am. I am one with God."

And no one can do that for you. You have to do that for yourself.

Living with that understanding is my greatest sadness, but also my greatest joy. As a counselor and healer, my human sadness is that I cannot help them with more than wise guidance and compassion. As a teacher, I experience immense joy when I see women take these teachings and free themselves from their own prisons.

They won't get out of the prison without a knowledge that there is a world outside, another way for them to live. And then they have to experience that outside world and find out it's safe. Safe because they are aware and strong within themselves.

That's why I hold retreats for women.

First I help them blow away the old myths of who women are and who men are. I suggest to them how they can relate differently to each other. They gain new knowledge about who they are and who they can be. Then they learn tools to help them get there and maintain themselves. All the while, they are using those tools and experiencing themselves as powerful, compassionate women.

By the time they leave, they have a seed of the new woman planted and sprouting in themselves. They have a daily program to help that little plant grow and thrive. That's why so many women come back to retreat after retreat, to keep nurturing the person they are becoming.

What does the wise woman do in the case of judgement?

She must remain free of judgement. If it comes up, her response is to inspire, elevate, and uplift.

What if her man judges her? Inspire, elevate and uplift. If she judges him? Stop it. Inspire him, elevate him, uplift him. And if he continues judging her and will not stop, no matter what she does? Then she has to leave. It is abuse, torture, devaluing.

Each woman must retain her value in the relationship. Without it, the relationship cannot live. If she lives very long with his negativity, it will feed into her propensity for self-doubt. She will absorb it like a sponge. It will weaken her energy fields, one by one, until her nervous system collapses, her immune system goes down, and she becomes mentally and/or physically ill.

A woman who holds on too long in a negative relationship can die.

Why do you think the cancer rate is rising so rapidly among women, as well as the rate of heart attacks? Because women internalize rage, and rage throughout the world is mounting astronomically. Women try to ignore it, rationalize their way around it, and hold on too long. They are catching the rage just like a disease.

Strokes used to be the big killer of women. Strokes are a slow disease; they build slowly over the years, feeding on internal frustration, doubt, worry and anger over little things they cannot change. And then some little blood vessel cannot hold a speck of something and it bursts.

Heart attacks and cancer are born from rage. Rage generated by a life they cannot change, based on lessons they brought in with them from past lives, often with the same people around them. This is the science of energetics' understanding of what is called a genetic predisposition for cancer. Add to that the rage they got growing up with father, mother, brother, boyfriends and partners. After eating so much rage it becomes their rage.

You are what you eat and you eat what (and who!) you live with. You become so stuffed, so full if it, that you cannot digest it and eliminate it – colon cancer. The pressure becomes so great that the blood vessels plug up with it – arteriosclerosis – and there is no light or fresh blood that can pass through them. Where's the joy? And then one straw too many breaks the camel's heart.

Is there a way out of this prison, this hell to which we continually contribute more bricks and mortar for even stronger walls? Yes. How?

You must commit to a new way of life. Not because you fear death, but because you value your life above all else.

There is a new Eden for every Adam and Eve, but they have to enter it one by one. In other words, you must take yourself there first. Do not wait for your partner, your mother or father, your children. Do not spend time trying to persuade and cajole them. If you go there, others may follow on their own, perhaps even inspired by you. But you must go alone, whether or not they will ever go themselves.

We as women came here to deliver this Earth, this humanity from its prison. We have to deliver ourselves first. Then all the cords connecting us with the old ways, the old deaths, and death itself will be severed. Forever.

Now let us walk that path to Eden together. The path of excellence and grace. The path of Womanheart.

12

THE PATH TO EDEN

*God did not promise you
that you would achieve Eden.*

That you have to do for yourself.

The Path to Eden

Life is a series of choices committing us to an ever-changing path. Each choice alters our path slightly and all choices made meld together as our life path. Even if we think we avoid choice, or choose not to choose at some point, that too is a choice and alters our path.

The path you walk is in reality a multiplicity of intertwined paths, some paralleling yours for awhile and then intersecting, others coming in at a diagonal and traveling with you for awhile and then veering off.

Each path that joins yours is some experience, represented by many things - a person, a new job, an event you may call a success or failure.

Your path is a composite of all that you have learned by living through all those experiences. In some places, the path resembles a brick road, or even strong cement, standing firm against opposition; in other places it flows like a river, flexing swiftly around objects in its way.

You are not the path. You are the soul that makes choices and accumulates these experiences, walking the road until the lessons are learned (hopefully!) and you no longer need this life.

At any point, you and your path can enter Eden.

The following is paraphrased from many comments about this made by Yogi Bhajan based on the most ancient, sacred knowledge.

God promised your soul several things before it came in to occupy this precious human life form. God promised you a mother and a father, but with no promise that they would "be there" for you as you might wish them to be.

Most importantly, God promised you two paths and an unlimited number of opportunities to chose between them throughout your life. One came with the appropriate major lesson you came to learn in this lifetime – this is the path called your karma. If you master it, great! But you have to come back in again with another karma and lesson to learn.

Then there was the promise you were given that there would be another path with a lesson on it you *might* learn, and if you learned it that would free your soul from the cycle of ongoing deaths and rebirths. That path is called your Dharma or Destiny.

God also promised you that you would meet your spiritual teacher sometime in your lifetime, one who would help to point the way to the Destiny Path, which flows through Eden on the way to eternal rest.

But God did not promise you that you would recognize that teacher or, even if you did, that you would follow what that teacher said and do what that teacher said to do. In other words, God did not promise you that you would achieve Eden.

That you have to do for yourself.

BRINGING OUT THE GOD

Every one of us – every man and every woman – has God within them. The question is: how do we bring out the God in ourselves, in someone else, in the man we love or the child we brought into this world?

You cannot bring out the God in anyone until you bring out the good. And you cannot bring out the good in yourself until you are willing to work to bring it out in someone else. And the more you commit to and do that, for as many people as you know, the more goodness comes out in you. The more you become like God.

So what brings out the good in someone? Words attached to the vision of goodness. Words that heal and uplift. Words that touch the heart.

Throughout the centuries, ladies of the royal court were taught to speak courteously, full of praise, for their men. And those men rode out to bring back triumphs for those who praised them.

To do that, those ladies had to come from their hearts.

That is how they came to be known as "gentle women," because they helped to create "gentle men."

Yet coming from your heart isn't easy. It doesn't come by giving away your heart – and you know how easy it is to do that. Giving away your heart is part of the falling-in-love formula we talked about in earlier chapters.

Instead, you have to come from your heart.

Try as hard as you may to come from your heart, you cannot do that on your own, stimulated only from the inside.

You and your persona project out from primarily one chakra or energy center at any given time. From the inside, you can move pretty easily from first, second and third chakras, stimulated largely from within yourself.

When you are in primary survival mode, you project strongly from the first energy center – men do this easily. When women are most needy and feel themselves failing to survive, they come from the first center. When you are in cozy-cutsie mode you are coming from the second chakra. When you seek to establish your identity and command respect you come from the third.

Moving up to the fourth, or heart, center is not done easily from just internal desires. You can actually jump over the heart and get into the throat chakra or above that into a more world-expanded frame - all from your own internal doing. But without the heart, you are in pieces, not at peace.

Thinking sweet thoughts will not get you into your heart - more likely you'll jump right down into the second sexual energy center. Reading or looking at sweet or pleasant things may bump you up into your higher centers but you'll be spacey.

An easy way to get into your heart is to talk to someone else's heart. Then you'll move into your heart quite naturally.

THE SACRED CENTER

There is another way.

The heart is the sacred center of the human, the place where the soul comes to rest when it first enters the body. It is the natural home for the soul. A person who we think of as compassionate, empathetic, merciful, comes from their heart.

So what is the sacred center of your life?

Your mind will tell you it is many places, depending on the pressures you're under at any given time, or the imaginative reach of your mind at times when pressures lessen.

Mind will tell you that your husband or lover is your sacred center. But how can you let it be outside you? How will you be safe? If so, you can lose your center if that other person moves away.

So it stands to reason that your sacred center should be in you. Your soul sits at your heart center, why not sit there with your soul?

Come to know your soul as your best friend – that's the best way to come from your heart.

Meditate on your heartbeat and know your friend, your one great friend. It will give you the ultimate in self-confidence. It will give you the experience of the Great Self within you and a union with what we call God.

A woman holds the sacred center of a marriage, a home. She has to live as that sacred center to maintain the fluxes and flows of energy of her husband, children, all those who live in or enter her home.

How does she do that?

By creating a sacred center for her own self in her home.

Let me share the story of a couple in trouble and the woman who created a miracle in their lives by doing just this thing.

She was the wife of a lawyer, the mother of a beautiful 10-year-old girl, college-trained herself and a leading member of her community, a role model for many women. Few among even them had any inkling of the private hell she had lived for years with her marriage.

When she first came to me, I was shocked by the stories of shouting and rage, even pushing, shoving and occasional bruising that happened between this picture-perfect husband and wife. Didn't they have everything to be thankful for, to live for?

No. In her words, she had "lost it" years before. She had lost her cool with him, and as I quickly discovered she had lost her center, her spirit and spiritual base with herself and her God.

She still did her daily prayers as many classically-reared Oriental women do from childhood up, but the practice and the passion for it had dwindled under the pressure of "keeping up" with their neighbors and other peers. Democratic as we American-born like to think our country is, all émigrés here have a tough row to hoe to gain education and recognition and be viewed as equals by their similarly educated friends and professional associates.

When I first met her, her eyes struck me. She had the look of a sad little bird, with big soft eyes that could melt the hardest heart. Her husband had a strong jaw, piercing eyes and nervous lines across his forehead.

She told me she was afraid to sleep with him, sometimes even afraid to be in his presence in the living room. And their daughter experienced continual stomach cramping before each evening meal, anticipating the fighting that ensued nightly over the food.

"I don't know what to do to stop him," she said, tears streaming out amidst the words. "I've lost it. I shout back at him when he shouts, even when he doesn't shout, and then I lock myself in the bedroom and pray that he just goes away, or maybe even dies, and I know that's horrible."

"Have you tried spending some quiet time together, being cozy, and talking about what's happening?" I asked.

"We never get time together. He's always busy and I always have our daughter and her friends to drive around or meals to cook."

"What would it take for you to put time aside, just for each other, to do something pleasant together?"

"Perhaps a miracle. He doesn't even want to be with me now, only sometimes for sex. And I hate it when he has sex with me, he's so rough."

Things had obviously gone too far to use logic or sweet talk. So I went right to the heart of the matter. Her spiritual core.

"Let's assume, for the moment, that you can't help him to change, okay?" She nodded her head. "So let's help you for now. Sound good?" She smiled faintly.

I gave her a meditation to do for 11 minutes each day, in the morning or evening, whenever she could be alone, and asked her to come back to see me in two weeks. I asked God for a miracle – not the kind she had asked for, but the kind that clears the mental debris and brings one back to center. Until she could get there, it would not be possible for her to see clearly her position and make a conscious decision as to whether or not she should stay with him.

Conventional counselors might look at the facts – the psychological abuse and occasional shoving encounters – and urge the woman to leave immediately. In her cultural base, however, divorce is shunned, and the woman who takes such action lives with a great degree of guilt.

When I saw her next, the first thing I saw was the change in her skin color – rosier cheeks – and twinkling lights in her eyes. There were still tears, but she could speak out for longer periods before her eyes would start to cloud up and get dark. The light of the soul had turned back on.

"I've done it every day, even though it was hard!" she announced proudly as soon as she sat down across from

me. *"I like the way it makes me feel, even when I cry during the chanting. I keep going and, just like you said, the tears pass. When I finish I feel more peaceful."*

"Great," I responded, reflecting her joy. *"Now I have a question. Where did you do the meditation – where in your home did you do it?"*

"Well, anyplace I could find that was not in use. Does it matter?"

"Yes it does. It doesn't have to be a fancy place, some special room. But it has to be a place that is just for your use at that time. Not some place like your bedroom or living room where people could walk in at any time unannounced. Do you have such a place?"

"Maybe the guest room."

"Fine. Then use it for this purpose, continue the meditation for another two weeks and then come see me again."

Before she left I also taught her a special de-stressing breath to use once or twice during the day. She learned it quickly.

Now lest you think it strange that someone should have to have a special place just to meditate, let me explain. You can meditate anywhere, anytime, hopefully alone or with others who are also meditating. In fact, you can meditate silently even when others are around as long as you don't have to interact with them.

So why did I ask this lady to adopt a special place to do her meditation?

Because she had no boundaries, no comfort zones, and didn't know how to establish them. That means, she didn't know how to protect herself. Because of that, he was always in her face and she had no place to retreat to. In other words, she had no "home" for herself in her own home.

By giving her this pre-condition to her meditation, this became a simple way to help her create such a space for herself and, at the same time, make it a special place where she would feel cozy, special and even sacred.

Next, I had to work on how she perceived herself and, it would follow, how he perceived her.

Based on her own descriptions to me, it seemed obvious that he saw her as a whiner, complainer, overloaded-with-duties Mom. Not much inspiration in that for either of them.

How to change that?

"Your husband is a pillar in your church community, am I right?" I asked her at our next meeting.

"Yes. He does everything there is to do. But I know he doesn't really believe in God. Not really."

"And does he lead the prayer before dinner at home?"

"Yes, well most of the time. Sometimes he forgets." She looked a little sideways at me, a look fearing judgement in her eyes.

"No matter. He's used to being the one who does it, yes?" She nodded her head. "Okay. I'd like you to suggest at the table tonight that your daughter sometimes be the one to lead the prayer and sometimes you will too. In fact, suggest it be on sequential nights. First he does it, then you, then your daughter, then back to him."

"But I don't understand..."

I took her hands in mine and squeezed them. "Just trust me. Let him lead in a sacred task and then you and your daughter join in. It will make a difference. Perhaps small at first, but over time it will help him to see you in a different light."

She mentioned that they were moving into their new home that weekend.

"Is there a room for you in that new home?" I asked.

"No. But I can make one, using the guest room as mine."

That would be easy, she said, as this home was a much larger home than their present home. So I took a great leap, hoping she would follow.

"Does your husband agree with your religious beliefs that God lives in every heart and in every home?" She nodded in agreement. "Then tell him you want to set aside one room for prayer and meditation, and put your scripture in there where you can read it every day. It doesn't need to be a large room."

"But he would think it was a waste. He has every room already designated for some purpose."

"Then tell him he will set a precedent for others at his temple, and this room will also be for his use as well as for you and your daughter's use."

She nodded her head as she mulled it over. "There is a small area off the downstairs sitting room we don't know what to do with. We thought maybe we could make it into a large closet for storage."

"Can you make it into a beautiful, special space?" I asked.

"Yes, I can."

"And will you meditate there and read scripture each day?"

"Yes."

"Then you have a chance to change your home and your life with him. Go do it!"

I knew that she had a chance with him if she could change her perception of herself in her own eyes and in his. That would take a steady daily practice, and spiritual practice could win him over - win over first his ego and pride that his wife was doing something so special, and eventually win over his soul to a happier path.

Did it work? Yes, slowly but surely.

She took the lead and established the sacred center in the home. He gradually followed. After two months of her doing this steadily, one of the women in her community told her (with no small amount of envy) that she had heard about these wonderful things that she was doing and how proud her husband was of her, telling various people in the community about her.

He even came in to join her when she read scripture and took time to read some on his own. Their daughter sat peacefully with them both when they read and prayed together.

People began to notice happy changes in them both, and she noticed the returning gentleness in him.

Could such a cure work for anyone? Yes. You can call your room the meditation center or "the place where I do my stuff." Even if you relate to no scripture, hold no book as especially sacred to you, that doesn't matter. Just sit there each day and meditate aloud. Your sound and your presence will spread that sacred space throughout the house, touching everyone within it.

Now there is one caveat to this process I must mention. When you create change on this subtle yet profound level, others who live with you will have only two options by way of response. At some point they will exercise one of them: change and come up to a higher place... or move along.

Can you predict which way it will go? No, not even given the best of situations. But rest assured, every woman who meditates regularly has God sitting protectively right by her shoulder. Whatever happens will be for her best.

Is this then the cure for every battered woman still in relationship? No, not all the time. Sometimes the breakdown has gone too far, the partners do not share common spiritual values, or the man has not made a sacred marriage commitment to her.

This is, however, the process by which the woman can raise herself up and break the pattern of abuse. As to her partner, well... you can provide an opportunity but, of course, you can never guarantee the outcome. Some stubborn horses led to water still may not drink.

It is important to become the divine human, and this is a simple but time-tested successful process for achieving that. You can go to churches and temples all your want, do all the rituals and sacred things that others say to do. But if you can't bring God into your sacred center, your home, then nothing else will work. Because when you do that, *you* work.

So does that mean we have to ascribe to some religion for this to work? No. Anyone can establish a sacred center without having to think of it as coming from God. Maybe you think of the source of all things as Divine Order, or you refer to "Universe does this or that" in your life. Maybe the objects you place at your sacred center aren't regarded by anyone as a scriptural text – simply a book of poetry that inspires you. These objects are only reference points for you that allow you to align yourself with your inner sacredness.

BECOMING FULLY HUMAN

How many times have you heard someone say, "If only I could be God for a day!"? They mean, of course, if only they had the powers of God to create abundance for themselves or get out of trouble.

That is only *playing* God. It doesn't work. Ask anyone who is truly wealthy, and they will tell you, perhaps only privately, that they still have their miseries.

Why? Because most people put the wrong thing first. We didn't come here to be all-powerful God, the Great Doer. We came here to be human. That is why we are called human beings, not human doers.

So what is a human being? The one who is a friend to his soul, who lives as the "light of the soul" (remember the definition of human?) in the human body.

Does the soul judge people? No. The personality does. Does the soul feel anger, revenge? No. Does the soul get neurotic, feel abandoned? No. But the personality does. And as it does all this more and more, it clouds over the soul, making it heavy so to speak. And the human loses touch with the soul.

Being in touch with the soul you can be human and, so elevated, live as God. What does living as God mean?

Let me share with you part of the opening of a prayer I do every day called the "mool mantra" that takes us to our core as divine humans. It presents all the basic aspects of God and challenges us to awaken them within ourselves.

Here are the words, in the ancient Sanskrit language.

"Ek Ong Kaar, Sat Naam, Kartaa Purakh, Nirbhao, Nirvair, Akaal Moorat, Ajoonee, Saibhang, Gur Prasaad. Jaap!" The translation is: "The Creator of all is One; Truth is His Name. He is the Doer of Everything. He is Fearless, Without Anger. He is Undying, Unborn, and Self-Illumined. This is revealed by God's Grace. Meditate!"

It closes with "Aad Sach, Jugaad Sach, Hai Bhee Sach, Naanak Hosee Bhee Sach!" This translates: "He was true in the beginning. He was true through all the ages. He is true even now. Guru Nanak says He shall ever be true!"

Repeating this chant in the ancient language over days, weeks, months gradually attunes the vibratory rate of the human to the divine frequencies. I have watched it happen to thousands who chant it daily and whose lives become fully human, the light of the soul.

Only when you can be fully human can you live as God. Because in that state of sublime humanness, you move into Divine Action, and then you are living God on Earth.

You get to the state of consciousness called "God and me, me and God are one" – one of the few English chants Yogi Bhajan has given us. And then all things are possible through you, all your actions at that time are living God. Then the big challenge is staying there.

Does that mean you lose your individuality at that time, so to speak, your sense of you?

Definitely not, though many fear this. There are people who try to expand or alter their consciousness to become something that is not them. No matter how hard they try, they can never completely become something which is not already within them.

They are looking for God outside themselves, rather than seeking to awake the God qualities already within them, carried by their soul.

These are the consequences of trying to become God without focusing on being fully human. As long as you focus on something outside you, you will never own it. You will believe in God only by faith but without experience.

Instead of spending your time trying to become God – God as someone else has defined it for you – focus on becoming fully human. In this way the God qualities will awaken within you.

This is the only route by which God can become personal to you. You awaken God within you.

No one can ever destroy your personal God because this is living God to you. All you have to do to keep that personal God alive is talk to him or her each day. Use the mantra! It works. And there are others like it that continue to expand the God within you.

And as for the possibility of losing yourself, it can never happen with this process.

Remember the early chapter where we talked about the ten energy bodies that surround the soul while it lives in human form? The subtle body is the individual's multi-lifetime informational hard drive. As long as it is with you, you retain your past memories, your karmas, your portrait of self.

So what is the process to become fully human and live God? And how do we get there?

THE SCIENCE OF THE SACRED NAME

Something that can help you speed toward this goal and achieve your destiny is asking a spiritual teacher for a sacred or spiritual name. This is entirely different than creating your own special name. There are a few rare teachers in the world who can see your destiny.

One great teacher who can do this is Yogi Bhajan. The names he gives, when chanted and used to address someone, awakens the destiny within that person and moves them in that direction.

You learn how to chant using your name. It took me a long time to realize just how precise a tool for self-upliftment the sacred name can be. It is truly a key to awaken the full human and unlock the destiny. I think of it as a name-key.

My name-key – Sangeet (pron. "Sun-geet") – means Divine Music or, in the realm of human relations, it means one who brings peace and harmony.

How does that work? When I chant my prayers in the ancient Sanskrit language of Gurmukhi each morning and quite literally become divine music throughout my ten energy bodies, my cat comes running from wherever he is to sit in my lap. Even my little parrot jumps and dances in ecstasy. By my doing that simple act, changing my frequencies, it is possible for me to spread peace and harmony to others I see as a healer and counselor during the day.

Another sacred name-key, Amarsharan, means one who is protected by the Infinite. The woman with this name has to vibrate the Infinite each morning with her meditations. In this way, she remembers her great protector and doesn't lean too heavily on her husband and others.

A man named Hari Nam has to manifest from the place of God-creativity, the Har, so he has to be in new creative mode at least once a day. Then he is aligned with his center. Creative also means playful, explorative. And for a man that's important – man the great explorer.

The sacred name helps you to live in your highest vibrations. Even if you don't have such a name, chanting the mool mantra and others in that ancient language will put you into the highest vibrations.

ACHIEVING THE HIGHEST VIBRATIONS

If you want to live in the highest vibrations, there are some things you will have to stop doing, as quickly as you can.

As you chant in this ancient language, you awaken God within. You listen to the highest sounds of God.

You cannot hear these sounds if your vibration is too heavy. It's not about how much you weigh. It's about being able to move these highest sounds through you. Some things will muffle the sounds to the point where you cannot hear them.

What things? Things that you put into yourself – into your mind and body.

For instance, if you fill your mind with so-called entertainment that is full of violence and rage, your mind will have no room to hear higher sounds. If you gossip, talk or think harsh thoughts about yourself or others, all you will be able to hear is the gibberish and fears of the lower mind.

Similarly, if you fill your body with foods that require continual processing and slow down or even block higher flows, you will also be unable to hear those higher vibrations.

Think about what happens when you really overeat. You want to sleep. This is hardly a state for higher conscious meditation!

Some foods even create conflicting sounds in your body. When you eat flesh foods – meat, fowl, fish – the vibrations in your body become heavy as it labors continually to try to digest and eliminate them. Waste materials accumulate from these foods that are never completely eliminated, producing a growing sluggishness.

Eat cheese and wheat gluten and listen to the slowing heavy sounds of the giant colon. Eat sugar and caffeine and hear the scream of the liver, the whine of the kidneys drying up and ringing in your ears as you age, and the freaky sound of the high-pitched nervous system as it makes you jumpy, sending erratic signals throughout your body.

Then you cannot resist tears, fears and angers. You are living in all the wrong vibrations and you cannot hear the highest ones – the highest You.

You finally recognize that something is wrong when it becomes pain – pain of arthritis from the drying cracked joints of your stored anger. Pain of the dried up kidneys from your stored frustrations. And the voice of pain is horrid.

Yet even within that pain you may hear another voice screaming through it all – "O my God, My God help me!" And that voice wants to connect to the soul.

Change now and come to life.

Eat living foods, not death. Eat what doesn't consume you. Eat nothing that had a Mother, and you will rise to your highest. God shall come to life in you.

You were made to remember God within and live God. You are never alone, never without, never rejected or abandoned. But if your soul cannot vibrate through you, God seems far away to you. And you cannot vibrate with your soul if you cannot hear it.

The soul sits in the heart. So listen to your heart, hear the sound of God within the sound of the heart. That's the key. Do it every day and every day shall be yours.

Here is a picture of how one such woman changed her life with her morning yoga and meditations. She first experienced it at a Womanheart Retreat. After several months, she talked to me about her experiences at length.

This is her story.

SADHANA

*She sits quietly on the floor in the darkness of her room,
her legs crossed under her, her spine straight, her hands
resting on her knees. It is two hours before dawn when
the sun is only a thought far below the horizon.*

*Outside in the darkest darkness of the night, the Earth
has fallen into a deep hush, that strange quiet before
the first chirpings of birds and the rise of the first wind,
announcing the oncoming day.*

*Inside this little room she is, and is not, aware of that
outside stillness. Because she is, and is not, there. One
could examine her body, since that is indeed present in
this room. Were there light, it would be obvious from
the sweat on her brow that she has been exercising her
body. Her form is the most ancient of all yogas
incorporating breath techniques that cleanse and purify
body and mind.*

*The room around her is filled with the sound of a long
powerful chant she has been toning for several minutes.
The tone has quieted her mind and carried her soul far
beyond this room.*

*Following the tunnel of light in front of her, streaming
out from that portal known since ancient times as the
third eye, she has gone far beyond charted space. At
times she sees the lights ahead stream past her like a
starship traveling through space.*

*Centuries ago, the mystic Plotinus called this state the
flight of the alone to the alone." Saint Theresa called it
"the house of many doors."*

But to her, it is simply the act of "going Home.". It is a way of finding peace and consuming that ultimate soul-food that will make each day on this planet for her more beautiful.

After awhile she will return to awareness of her body and to the stirrings of the world outside, to her duties to others within her house and the cares of the day ahead.

This practice she engages in each morning in the pre-dawn hours is an ancient one called "sadhana." It means "daily spiritual practice." It may be the most selfish act one can do, focusing on the vibrations of the soul to reach the God within. But with this one selfish act at the start of each day, this woman will grow in strength, grace and courage.

Over time using this sadhana, she will experience and live a life of selflessness for the balance of that day and God will cover her and her actions.

How can this be? Somewhere within her sadhana there will be a few precious moments – even if in Earth time that may be only seconds – that will bring her to that "peace which passes all understanding," an expression in a prayer she remembered reciting during her childhood.

Once touched by that, her day, and her life, will be forever changed. Repeating it, she will gradually come into a steadiness and mental neutrality that will enable her to live by one principle: never react. Never react to her fears, angers, hard words, and never react to those of others. That is the only way one can stop the cycle of re-action – the human chain reaction – that is tearing life apart.

Without reaction there cannot be war. Without reaction there is a chance for love.

She is giving herself that chance, one day at a time, by doing this sadhana.

She learned this form of sadhana from a Kundalini Yoga teacher who shared with her many aspects of the yoga lifestyle as taught by Yogi Bhajan.

When she began doing sadhana she had just turned 40 years old. She had thought it was too late for her, too late to change her life from the grit and grime of hopelessness and an everyday job and a long line of meaningless lovers. She thought she could never stop the incessant chattering of her mind, the mental imagery and worries that played on her internal television screens, and the doggerel of vague dreams.

Over the first forty days of doing a simple sadhana that took her only 20 minutes each morning, she found herself frequently tempted to stay late in bed. But she conquered those temptations and, sleepily, dressed in her sweats, went out into her living room. After awhile she found that keeping up kept her up, just as her teacher had told her.

Gradually, there were other signs of change in her life. On the way to work, she found herself lightly hopping up on the bus steps instead of dragging herself up them. Several times during the day she caught herself smiling as she worked, smiling for no particular reason, and in an atmosphere of stress where no one ever smiled except at some bad joke.

When someone rushed into her office with yet one more demand, she found herself observing and not caught up by the rush of blood flowing into her cheeks and, instead, taking a deep breath to quiet the stress before responding. Her words became calmer. People were beginning to notice and wonder what was happening. Perhaps she was in love.

There was truth in that speculation, but not about an earthly love. She was experiencing a higher love. In her daily sadhana she was replacing a flagging faith in God implanted in her by parents who, like most parents, thought faith was all that was needed. She was gradually replacing that faith with experiences of God in herself and herself in God.

What was happening was nothing short of miraculous. Where so many other women were seeking to gain confidence and self-esteem to bolster their feelings of powerlessness and poor position in job and family, she began to gain a far rarer commodity – self-trust.

Each day she continued her sadhana, she gained new insights into herself and others, new perspectives and new wisdoms. Her practice grew longer, the meditations sweeter and more compelling. Soon she found herself enjoying an hour, then even more. Gradually, she came to trust herself, to rely on those insights and her own steadiness.

She remembered a dedication that author William Faulkner had written to his mother at the start of his book, "As I Lay Dying." It read: "To my Mother, who not only survived, but prevailed."

As the weeks grew into months of a steady spiritual practice, she came to appreciate the distinction Faulkner had made. Survival was when you won out over great odds but you knew the battle to stay alive was never over. Prevailing over life meant that you could trust yourself to come through with love and values intact and not have to cling to life – in fact, to stand and fight for them and die for them if necessary. The love and the courage to live with those values were more important than the life itself.

And she was also learning another valuable lesson. She was learning how to give herself inner kindness, how to like herself and do good things for herself. This is far from indulgence. It is the milk from which comes the practice of giving kindness to others.

Those who do not like themselves and show it to themselves daily, do not have the ability to truly like others, let alone love them.

She was no longer one of them.

Great women aren't born. They're created right here on Earth. They're forged by the crucible of challenges, enormous challenges – and by facing them day by day, by never surrendering to their fears and tears, they make themselves great.

How do you make a diamond? Never the easy way.

And once you begin the process, you cannot stop. Challenges will come, and you must not waiver in your continuing process of self-transformation. That way, you bring hope to not only yourself but to others you love.

It will help you through the darkest times.

FIRST PRINCIPLES

Sadhana is the act done to honor the first principle of a spiritual life: know yourself and your God within you. The unwritten "law" to be obeyed is:

**Soul shall rise before sunrise
and the day shall be yours!**

From that experience, practiced daily, come the other keys to the higher life, the Eden, expressed in these words: ***obey, serve, love, excel.***

Obey the inner teacher, the God within you.

Serve all selflessly.

Love without condition, without need.

Excel and experience the flow of God forever.

These are the first five keys to entering the place called Eden. Through the practice of sadhana in the early hours when all is quiet, you can connect with God.

This is how the steps work.

When you know yourself so sublimely, you then can know the inner teacher and thus you can obey the voice. Otherwise, you obey the ego.

When you can obey that inner teacher, then you can serve all selflessly, that is to say "serve the good in all" which leads to serving the God in all.

Then you can truly love without neediness, without conditions and with no reaction to your own emotionality or that of any one else.

Only when you can so love can you be free to experience your own excellence through the power of your own rising God energy, called kundalini. In this way you can experience God flowing through you forever.

Let's look closer at these principles and how to put them into action. Taken together, they form the foundation of a healthy yogic, spiritual lifestyle as recommended by Yogi Bhajan and practiced by thousands around the world.

First and most important: rise in the "ambrosial hours," as they are called, one to two hours before dawn, and do yoga and meditation in the practice of sadhana.

That means Get up! Those who sleep through dawn die a little each day. Their life becomes more and more driven by emotions - cluttered, meaningless, and painful.

Have you not heard how many spiritual pathways honor those special hours? Jews, Catholics, Muslims, Buddhists, and Sikhs who deeply live their practices all know the power that can come to you when you get up and do some sort of meditative practice in those hours.

So where and how do you start such a practice?

A NEW DAY DAWNS

First you start by turning off the nighttime television by, let's say, 9 p.m., setting the alarm for 5 a.m., setting out some warm clothes to put on when you get up, and then going to sleep by 10 p.m. so you can "answer the call" when the alarm goes off for the first time.

When you get up, prepare yourself with an invigorating cold shower. That's right – *cold*. It will give your cardiovascular and nervous systems a thorough flush and cleanse as nothing else can. Nothing ages you faster in the morning than a warm shower.

The shower routine is pretty simple. Rub a few drops of almond oil all over your body. Then turn the faucet on to full cold and step in, first wetting your legs, then arms, then face, and finally your torso. All the while, rub yourself vigorously. Then step out, still rubbing yourself all over. Step back in and really get soaked while still rubbing, then step out again. The third time you step in, you most likely won't feel the cold anymore. When you finish, you'll have a nice red glow and feel very much alive!

Then choose a place to do some simple yoga and meditation. Put a natural fabric on the floor to sit on. Have a nice warm shawl or small blanket to put over you when you meditate.

Now here comes the most important suggestion: don't bite off more than you can chew. In other words, don't start out with a daily routine that lasts an hour or more – believe me, you won't last longer than a few days. Start modestly.

Of the thousands of Kundalini Yoga sets I've done and taught over the past twenty years, I'm suggesting here something that will only take you about 10 to 12 minutes, followed by a simple meditation that can be as brief as 12 minutes or as long as 30 minutes.

It will help greatly if you find a Kundalini Yoga teacher in your area. You want to learn how to properly tune in to the golden chain of Kundalini Yoga masters with this chant at the start of every yoga set: *Ong Namo Guru Dev Namo* (I bow to the Creator, I bow to the wisdom within me and beyond me).

The teacher can also guide you in doing the postures and movements and in the correct pronunciation of the meditation: *Saa Taa Naa Maa* (which translates roughly as existence, birth, death, rebirth).

Kundalini Yoga is the oldest of all yogas, and the purest teachings have been handed down to us by the current master, Yogi Bhajan. Be sure you chose a certified teacher from his 3HO organizations' Kundalini Research Institute (KRI). Contact information is in the *Resources to Explore* chapter.

THE CYCLE OF CHANGE

Do this sadhana for 40 days without missing a day and you will drop old habits and establish a new you. How? A goodly majority of our cells replace themselves every 40 days, so by doing this positive routine for 40 days you break old patterns in yourself and establish a new awareness of who you are deep in cellular memory.

If you miss a day, then you missed re-imprinting a whole flock of new cells. So you have to start again at day one. That's not arbitrary or punitive. That's simply the way the ancient science of human energetics works.

Well, there you have it – your first major step to opening the door to Eden.

You can use it or not. The choice will always be yours.

When you have done your beginning sadhana for a few weeks, you could ask your yoga teacher if he or she and others in the area do a regular sadhana which you could attend. Doing sadhana with others makes you stronger and amplifies the effects on everyone. A full sadhana is about two hours long and will inspire you. But don't attempt to do it yourself right away. Your own sadhana is a good start.

When you're ready for more, get a yoga manual and do a longer set. Ask your teacher to demonstrate it, or follow a set taught in class. Buy a sadhana meditation CD - there are many available - and do one or two of the chants. You can ask the teacher for a pronunciation sheet for the words. They are easier learned sung than spoken.

Next, you might want to do a short meditation before going to bed at night. It will make resting easier and gradually release you from the clutches of disturbing dreams. There are several meditations available on CD set to sweet melodies. You might do one for 11 minutes, 22 or 31 minutes.

So if you do a sadhana for 40 days will you like yourself more?

Yes, and it will continue to grow over time. Soon you will experience moments of peace during the day, and then longer times of contentment accompanied by feelings of elation, new vitality and stamina.

All who would become masters in this life must take these first steps each and every day.

<u>IMPORTANT:</u>

Before engaging in any exercise, including those that are in Womanheart, consult your health care professional. This publication is not intended to provide medical advice nor is it intended as a substitute for any treatment prescribed by your health care professional.

YOUR FIRST WOMANHEART SADHANA
(MEN CAN DO THIS TOO!)

Step One: Tuning In

This is always done at the start of any Kundalini Yoga set. It links you up to the power and protection of the golden chain of masters who have brought this ancient science to us down through the millennia.

Sit cross-legged on the floor, hands in prayer pose in the front of your chest at heart level (palm-to-palm). The end knuckles of both thumbs are pressed lightly into the sternum. Inhale and chant in one breath: **Ong Namo, Guru Dev Namo.** Repeat it two more times. At the end, take a long inhale, then slowly exhale.

Ong—   Namo—   Gu-ru Dev—   Namo—

Step Two: Warm-Up Spinal Flexibility Set

Nothing will assure youth and mental clarity better than maintaining flexibility of the spine. This set of exercises is a real winner. Breathe only through the nose, both on the inhale and exhale, in all positions.

1. Sit cross-legged. Hold on to shin of the outside leg. Flex the navel (and hips) forward on the inhale and back on the exhale, setting a steady
pace and doing this for **one minute**. End with a long inhale as you sit up straight, and a long exhale. Breathe only through the nose.

2. Then sit on your heels (use a pillow if this is difficult), and with hands resting on your thighs, continue flexing using the whole body
this time; inhale as you flex forward and exhale as you flex back. **One minute**. End with a long inhale and long exhale.

3. Bring your legs together straight out in front of you. Holding on to ankles or toes, inhale up and exhale down for **one minute**.

4. Again sit cross-legged. Put your hands on your shoulders, thumbs in back and other fingers in front, arms up parallel to the floor. Begin swinging the upper body and head from side to side. The head moves only with the body and no further. Inhale as you swing to the

left, exhale to the right. **One minute**. Then come to center and take a deep inhale and exhale before lowering arms.

5. With hands on knees, start shoulder shrugs. Inhale and raise both shoulders up toward the ears, exhale and let them drop (on the way down God does the work for you!) Continue at a steady pace for **one minute**. End with a long inhale and exhale.

6. With hands still on your knees, inhale, then exhale and drop the head forward so that your chin is resting on your chest. Start neck rolls slowly to the right, inhaling as you come across the back and exhaling as you roll slowly across the

front. Continue **circling seven times**, then **reverse the circle seven times**, continuing the same breath pattern. To end, bring the chin around to the center of the chest, inhale and raise the head up level, then exhale.

Step Three: Saat Kriya

This will take you to your truth, your essence, as implied in the word "Saat". It helps the energy to rise up the spine and open the crown chakra (energy center) to reach out and make that link with Infinity.

The full chant, "Saat Naam," means the identity of Truth and is an ancient sound current name for God. Chanting it erases karma and opens the door for your destiny to come.

Sit on your heels (with the aid of a pillow as necessary). Bring your hands together, interlace all fingers with only the index fingers pointing up, and raise the hands up over your head. Keep arms as straight as possible, with inner elbows hugging your ears. (Imagine God has a string tied to your index fingers and is pulling them up for you – it takes the strain off you!) Then take a long inhale, exhale, inhale. On the next exhale, start with the audible sound "Saat" (rhymes with "but") while quickly pulling the navel back towards the spine and slightly up. Follow that immediately with the voiced sound "Naam" (pron. "nahm") as you release the navel.

Set a steady pace (not racing) as you continuously chant "Saat Naam". The Saat will be more powerful a sound because of the navel pull, while the Naam will be gentler and shorter as the navel releases. You will notice that on the navel pull with Saat your whole torso pulls up a couple of inches, dropping back down with the sound of Nam.

Focus on pulling the energy up as you pull the navel, feeling it rise up the central channel of the spine into the head and out the crown.

Continue this for **three minutes**. End with a long inhale, tightening all the muscles along your spine, hold, then exhale powerfully, pulling the navel back and feeling the flow of energy upward. Repeat this two more times. Then take a long inhale and slowly exhale as you lower your hands together into your lap. Relax for at least a full minute.

Step Four: Meditation to Kirtan Kriya
(pron. "Keertan Kreeya")

The title Kirtan Kriya means divine music. It takes the phrase you chanted earlier, Saat Naam, and breaks it into its five primary sounds – Saa Taa Naa Maa, with "aa" said to be the fifth sound common to them all. This meditation burns up karma and helps to lighten your load of past problems both remembered and stored deep in your subconscious.

Sit cross-legged, hands in gyan mudra (hands rest on knees, palms up, with index fingers touching halfway down the first joint of each thumb). Eyes are closed, rolled up under closed eyelids to focus at a point above the nose between the eyebrows known as the third eye.

It has been said that if you can keep your eyes controlled and focused on this point you can control your mind and drop the incessant chatter with which we are all familiar. Try it, it works. Of course, be prepared for a lot of chatter-static and self-talk in the beginning. That's part of the process of clearing out. Just keep chanting.

Start by chanting the four sounds Saa Taa Naa Maa over and over in a sing-song little tune (middle E-D-C-D). Take short inhales as you need to without stopping the rhythm of the chant. As you chant each sound, you press the thumbs to their respective fingers – first the index fingers, then the middle fingers, then the ring fingers and finally the little fingers. Keep up with this cycle for **3 minutes**. You are stimulating both hemispheres of the brain and all ten centers of the brain. It brings the greatest release-awakening you can have.

Next, continue moving the fingers but switch your voice to a strong whisper for **three minutes**. Then go into silence for six minutes. During the silence, keep the sounds going in your mind, keep your eyes focused on the third eye, and keep the finger sequence going. Come back out of the silence into the whisper and then the sung voice, **each for three minutes**. The entire meditation lasts for 18 minutes.

It's amazing how this meditation works. The fingers are the keyboard of the original – and still the greatest — computer, the human brain. Pressing them in this sequence excites energy flows in a specific pattern in the brain. Along with this mantra, this rhythmic pulsing and chanting can create beautiful change, de-stressing and releasing you from haunting thoughts, past worries and concerns.

The timing of this meditation is important. You can do it either in the 3-3-6-3-3 version (three minutes sung, three whispered, six in silence, three whispered and three sung) or you can do it in the five-minute cycle (5-5-10-5-5).

Don't be surprised if occasionally tears, other emotions, or worrisome thoughts come up. It's a strong "housecleaner." Just keep the chant going and you won't get stuck in any of the muck. It will be released forever!

WHO WE ARE BECOMING

We are the Women of Womanheart.

We walk with a smile, not a frown, so that the world may see the face of grace. We hold happiness as our birthright, and peace and harmony as our banner. We came to conquer the villains of fear and doubt, to put aside tears and fears. We came to live our excellence, to create trust and grow love.

We are the Women of Womanheart.

We came to be guiding stars. We came to be warmth where there is cold, strength where there is fear, laughter where there are tears. We came to be mothers and wives and daughters and sisters and Goddesses for all time. We came to serve and uplift humanity. We came from the Divine and we live in that glory every day.

We are the Women of Womanheart.

We are the first teachers and the first healers. We are the rekindlers of hope. We are the renewers of faith. We are the kindness in the heart that never dies. And in the end, our love and the remembrance of our love is the power that sends each child Home.

We are the Women of Womanheart.

We are becoming thousands, millions across this planet, and we are coming together as one. One hand to heal Mother Earth. One heart to nurture all. One path of excellence and grace.

We are the Women of Womanheart.

From dust to dust was not written of our soul. From dust to heaven is our goal.

13

RESOURCES TO EXPLORE

3HO & KUNDALINI YOGA

3HO stands for Healthy, Happy, Holy Organization which was founded in 1969 by Yogi Bhajan. It is now the largest yoga teaching organization worldwide and specializes totally in Kundalini Yoga as taught by Yogi Bhajan. 3HO's Kundalini Yoga teacher certification organization is known as "KRI" (Kundalini Research Institute).

For information on locating a "KRI"-certified Kundalini Yoga teacher and Kundalini Yoga classes in your area, visit the Kundalini Yoga web site at:

www.KUNDALINIYOGA.com.

Or call the Kundalini Yoga headquarters in Española, New Mexico, USA at: **1-505-753-0423**.

For information on 3HO's other events, courses, and workshops including international yoga festivals, Khalsa Women's Training Camp, and Kundalini Yoga Teacher Certification programs, visit their web site at:

www.3HO.org.

Or call 3HO at their headquarters in Española, New Mexico, USA at: **1-888-346-2420**.

The Kundalini Yoga and 3HO organizations are indispensable resources for everyone on the path of Womanheart. I encourage you to contact them at your earliest convenience.

WOMANHEART RETREATS

For an exciting adventure into the experience of Womanheart Healing Retreats for Women in Arizona, USA and elsewhere call Sangeet's office at The Healing Source, llc in Phoenix, Arizona, USA at:

1-888-WOMANHEART (that is 1-888-966-2643)

– or –   **1-602-265-9096**.

Take a tour of a Womanheart Retreat, learn more about Sangeet's teaching and healing work, and link-throughs to Kundalini Yoga books, meditations, music, videos, and other products by visiting the Womanheart web site at:

www.WOMANHEART.com.

The following excerpts from a recent brochure will give you additional insight into the Womanheart Retreat experience:

*O*pen Your Heart to Peace and Freedom

The Womanheart Retreat is a perfect way to transition into the real peaceful you and stay there. Womanheart helps you create inner courage and freedom while gaining valuable, life-long tools – all you need to prepare yourself for peace and calm.

There are fascinating lectures...

*M*ove to a New Life Rhythm

You are indomitable spirit. You are the heart of compassion and caring. You will move to a new daily rhythm so a whole new life can be yours. Rise each day just before dawn. Meditate in the beautiful outdoors and release limitations. Move with simple yoga, relax and free your body.

the spontaneity of group gatherings...

Lift your divine voice with ancient chants, releasing tears and bringing joy.

good vegetarian food,

*H*ealing Breath, Sacred Sound

Over four special days, your life will be vastly enriched and you will discover how to rise above even your darkest moments. You will gain a deeper understanding of *you* and how to create more loving relationships.

fun, and flowers...

You'll use the art of meditation and breath of life to take control of your mind and body. You'll connect deeply with your own soul. You learn about death, and help to release the souls of departed loved ones.

You will bask in the warmth and healing energy of a secluded, rustic retreat center in Arizona's high desert landscape, wrapped in the comfort and love of women from across the country.

things to ponder,

Mind, Body & Soul

Womanheart celebrates the whole woman. While delving deeply into the mind and soul, you'll also learn about the care and nurturing of your physical body. Enjoy dairy-free vegetarian cuisine that will nourish and refresh you.

personal sharing...

Lifelong Experience & Tools

Womanheart is life changing! But, what happens when you leave? This is the key to Womanheart. You leave with invaluable tools. You receive a daily program, designed uniquely for you, and only you.

and the peace of a moonlight meditation.

1-888-WOMANHEART
www.WOMANHEART.com

Womanheart Companion CDs with Sangeet Kaur Khalsa

Blessed with Bliss

Miracle Meditations
Volume One

Chanted & Sung by
Sangeet Kaur Khalsa

1. **Tuning In** – The Adi Mantra chanted three times links you to the golden chain of master teachers who have brought the ancient science of Kundalini Yoga and meditation down through the ages to us. The current master is Yogi Bhajan. Chant this mantra three times before doing any yoga set or meditation.

2. **Wahe Guru** – This is a very high mantra for self-transformation. Chanting Wahe Guru brings your destiny closer to you. This clears the darkness from the clouds in our hearts and helps us to avoid inherent danger. It also adjusts our perception of ourselves and helps us overcome feelings of poor self-worth. Practice for 120 days and keep going! You will get a feeling of vast horizons and feel young and energetic.

3. **Ra Ma Da Sa** - This is one of the oldest and highest healing chants. It can bring you out of all sickness on every level. It will expand you and glorify the self. It can be chanted in a group, in a healing circle, or alone by yourself.

4. **Guru Ram Das** - This chant brings phenomenal peace, protection and healing. It invokes the presence of one of the greatest Masters, Guru Ram Das, who brought to the people of 16th century India the ancient sciences of Kundalini Yoga and meditation and related healing abilities. Play the CD everywhere, most especially when you sleep.

5. **Longtime Sunshine** - Yogi Bhajan once commented that any yoga or meditation you do that begins with the Adi Mantra and ends with "Longtime Sunshine" can only work for your good. So use them both.

Womanheart Companion CDs with Sangeet Kaur Khalsa

Beyond the Beyond

Miracle Meditations Volume Two

Chanted & Sung by
Sangeet Kaur Khalsa

1. **Tuning In** – The Adi Mantra chanted three times links you to the golden chain of master teachers who have brought the ancient science of Kundalini Yoga and meditation down through the ages to us. The current master is Yogi Bhajan. Chant this mantra three times before doing any yoga set or meditation.

2. **Ong Namo Guru Deva** – This mantra quite literally tunes you in to the infinite wisdom. When you sit and chant it with total receptivity, see what universe with send you in new insights and wisdom. Do a 40-day practice and you will feel the expansiveness.

3. **Kirtan Kriya** – This is truly "divine music." It is a "bij" or seed mantra that helps erase karma and awakens your soul to its destiny. Chant it for 40 days and it will start to build a new and brighter you.

4. **Sat Narayan** – This chant can redeem you from all darkness and bring light into your physical presence and your life as well as good fortune and heightened intuition. Chant it and feel the joy as it brings truly great gifts.

5. **Longtime Sunshine** – Yogi Bhajan once commented that any yoga or meditation you do that begins with the Adi Mantra and ends with "Longtime Sunshine" can only work for your good. So use them both.

ABOUT THE AUTHOR

Sangeet Kaur Khalsa is a teacher, healer and counselor loved by thousands of women and their families whose lives she has touched both individually and in her Womanheart retreats over the past two decades. She was named "Woman of the Year 2000" for her life work as a healer and teacher by Arizona's leading YWCA. Although she has been based in Phoenix, Arizona since 1987, for more than 20 years prior to that she served as an executive with several top Fortune 500 companies in New York.

Sangeet has taught Kundalini Yoga and meditation for over 20 years and trained directly with renowned yoga master Yogi Bhajan. She has been a long-term member of the board of advisors of the International Kundalini Yoga

Teachers Association, and is a certified Kundalini Yoga teacher, a certified master NLP counselor and a respected Reiki Master-Trainer. Her white turban distinguishes her as a member of the Sikh faith which she also serves as a minister.

Sangeet's name literally means "Divine Music". In the human relations realm, it means "One who brings Peace and Harmony".